American Interior is not just a book: it is also an album, a film and an app:

THE ALBUM, released on Turnstile, features thirteen songs inspired by Evans's original journey, written in part on 2012's Investigative Concert Tour™.

THE FILM, directed by Dylan Goch, produced by ie ie productions, commissioned by S4C in association with Film Agency for Wales and distributed by Soda Pictures, is a visual document of the tour.

THE APP, published by Penguin, combines music, film clips, prose and animation in a unique, immersive version of the John Evans story.

Find out more about all of these at american-interior.com

Gruff Rhys is known around the world for his work as a solo artist as well as singer and songwriter with Super Furry Animals and Neon Neon, and for his collaborations with Gorillaz, Mogwai, Dangermouse and Sparklehorse amongst others. The latest album by Neon Neon, *Praxis Makes Perfect*, based on the life of radical Italian publisher Giangiacomo Feltrinelli, was recently performed as an immersive live concert with National Theatre Wales.

AMERICAN INTERIOR

The quixotic journey of John Evans, his search for a lost
tribe and how, fuelled by fantasy and (possibly) booze, he
accidentally annexed a third of North America;

or

Footnotes: a fantastical, musical quest in search
of the remains of Don Juan Evans

GRUFF RHYS

PENGUIN BOOKS

PENGUIN BOOKS

UK | USA | Canada | Ireland | Australia
India | New Zealand | South Africa

Penguin Books is part of the Penguin Random House group of companies
whose addresses can be found at global.penguinrandomhouse.com.

First published by Hamish Hamilton 2014
Published in Penguin Books 2015

001

Typeset in Fournier MT Std by Palimpsest Book Production Ltd, Falkirk, Stirlingshire
Printed in Great Britain by Clays Ltd, St Ives plc

A CIP catalogue record for this book is available from the British Library

ISBN: 978-0-241-96536-8

www.greenpenguin.co.uk

Cyflwynaf y llyfr hwn i Catryn, Mali Mai a Mabli

Chip chut R

Latitu

Beautifull
High Plain
upper
the Heer

Jupiter & fo
Bonedict Riv
150 yds w

upper end of }
Carp Island)

Lat by Observⁿ 49.
by Chart 46

47°..00..00 by Pole Star

Variation 1 P.t N.E

Casp R & Island

wintering ground
with the Rucarus

CONTENTS

Contents

Contents

PREFACE

When John Evans spent the summer of 1792 in London, it co-incided with Austrian composer Joseph Haydn's visit to the city to premiere his Symphony No. 97 in C major. It's unlikely that Evans was there, but certainly not impossible. However, it's another Haydn who is partly responsible for my intercontinental stalking of John Evans's shadow.

I first met Haydn in Detroit in 1999. He had driven heroically for six hours to come to a Super Furry Animals show at the Magic Stick, a bowling alley with a concert venue upstairs, next door to the hall where Houdini played his last trick. The famed escape artist died of peritonitis in a hospital across the road, having successfully freed himself from a straitjacket of chains whilst immersed in a glass tank of water. (The janitor took me to see the very spot.)

A passionate young man, Haydn had gathered a group of exiled Welsh youngsters together for a road trip to see their compatriots. He had come to America on a soccer scholarship to play for Rio Grande University, Ohio. Over the years he would turn up at shows as far afield as New York, Cleveland and Atlanta.

Conversations would usually turn to John Evans. Haydn had hit on a shared obsession. He was certainly the first person I met who wanted to recreate Evans's journey (although I think Haydn wanted to do it solely by boat). Beers were drunk and ideas hatched.

Every time we toured the US (around twice a year at the turn of the century), Haydn would plead, 'You have to visit Rio Grande; you won't believe it!' I certainly didn't, but now I do.

Gruff Rhys, 2014

INTRODUCTION

I n 1792 John Evans, a 22-year-old farmhand and weaver from the village of Waunfawr in the mountains of Snowdonia, Wales, responded to a plea from the great Welsh cultural mischief-maker Iolo Morganwg to settle, for once and for all time, the quandary of whether there was indeed a tribe of Welsh-speaking Native Americans still walking the Great Plains, descendants of Prince Madog, who was widely believed (especially by Welsh historical revisionists) to have discovered America in 1170.

With the aid of a loan from a gullible friend, Evans set sail to Baltimore to begin the greatest of adventures, whereupon he set off on foot and disappeared into the Allegheny Mountains with one dollar and seventy-five cents to his name, in search of the lost tribe.

Having undertaken the task of following Evans's journey by means of an investigative concert tour, I'd like to say here that all roads seem to lead back to my father, Ioan. During the reorganization of local government in 1974 the ancient realm of Gwynedd in North Wales was revived in name, and with ambitions to serve the land of Madog, my father really hit the jackpot – with a civil service post at Gwynedd County Council. Moving from South Wales, where his ancestors were steelworkers, innkeepers and preachers, Ioan and my mother, Margaret – a teacher with a sideline in poetry – settled my brother Dafydd, sister Non and me in the Welsh-speaking slate-quarry town of Bethesda, where we grew up, firmly protected by the colossal mountains of Snowdonia.

My father was a straight-talking, principled public servant and a dependable man, although further evidence points to a romantic streak that lay pretty close to the surface: a great mimic of animal noises, he once bought the original Lassie's grandson (granddog?) by mail order, and it arrived in a box at Dolgellau station. He called him Cafall, and the wise collie was his companion on mountain hikes, hypothetically ready to solve any crime mystery that would cross their path. My father was the subject of an MI6 file, as he was branded a Soviet sympathizer whilst a student at Harlech College, and in later life he taught himself German with a Swiss accent.

His mother, from whom he received his more magical attributes, was born Kate Parry just outside Waunfawr, fourteen miles from Bethesda. In her twenties, she reimagined herself as Kate Olwen. She had just died, and we were now returning to her domain. For reasons that no one fully understands, she was the only member of our family to play, or take any interest in, golf, and she once came last in the British Open. She was descended from John Evans's maternal uncle, Harri Dafydd, who was her great-grandfather, making John Evans her great-uncle.

My father used to tell me that, apart from me and my siblings, he and his cousin Mary Fôn were Evans's only living relatives – or maybe I misinterpreted him as a child, as from what I've since figured out, this isn't strictly true. I now know of a few others, and there must be descendants of his siblings dotted around the place; if they're anything like John, they could be anywhere.

Mary Fôn certainly helped to keep the John Evans flame alive too, and even went to America to search, unsuccessfully, for his grave. I remember visiting her bungalow as a seven-year-old. She gave me a huge conch shell from the Gulf of Mexico, which I was able to make some kind of trumpet sound with. I still have it on the side of my bath; my cats use it to sharpen their claws, and the same shell will appear on the soundtrack to the film of this book.

My father had started, in his spare time, to write books: Welsh-language guides on climbing the Welsh mountains; memoirs of his travels to various mountain ranges; a philosophical book on local governance, which somehow became a textbook at the University of Zambia; and eventually a greatest-hits package, *Bylchau* (which translates as 'gaps', 'passes' or even 'spaces'), which combined his love of mountains and his proto-anarchist political sympathies in one tome. He argued that the spaces between the mountains, the passes and the gaps where people and cultures meet, were more important and more interesting than the summits, the supposed pinnacles.

He was in the process of writing a lecture about Evans when he died, and had petitioned the governor of North Dakota with impassioned letters to get some recognition for his relative – a plaque in the Peace Garden State, at least, for Evans's stunts. Alas, to no avail, although in 1999 they did put up a beautiful slate memorial in Waunfawr. Meanwhile, my brother Dafydd took up the cause in the field of education and wrote two academic papers connected to Evans's influence on present-day American geography and the political similarities between European and North American minority languages.

I therefore grew up fantasizing that I was a direct descendant of John Evans and that his achievements and adventures were not only real but widely known by the general public. Did these tales have any basis in reality, however, or were they just elaborate bedtime stories? Now, as an adult, I began my journey of verification.

Living in Wales, an *almost* island, the seafaring Welsh have had an aptness for travel, yet have been, for the most part, short on resources.

This has led to some very imaginative thinking, with otherworldly results, bypassing the expense and hassle of maintaining, say, a populated space station. In the nineteenth century the Welsh colonized the impossible: the barren lands of Patagonia. In the same century things were so bad on the ground that they spent most of the time trying to colonize Heaven, where it was presumed Welsh was the official language. At the same time the heroic Chartist revolutionaries of 1839 imagined a better, fairer society for their children and were given free tickets to Australia.* As a Welsh pop musician I have been given a ticket to a lifestyle once afforded only to soldiers, Miss Universe contestants and long-distance truck drivers. Back in the eighteenth century, John Evans, however, went further into the beyond than was thought possible by even the wildest of Welsh dreamers.

Following the roads, the rivers and the epic trail of John Evans through the post-asphalt apocalypse of the American landscape, I will strive not only to create a fair picture of his place in history, but also to investigate how wild fantasies sometimes interact with hard history and how myth-making can distort real cultural identity and inspire humans to partake in the craziest, most vain pursuits of glory, including exploration, war and the creative arts.

* Convicted of high treason, the Chartist leaders of the Newport Rising were transported to Australia when their death penalties were commuted.

ACT ONE
THE YEAR OF THE TIGER

PRINCIPAL CHARACTERS

JOHN EVANS

A humble orphaned farmhand from Snowdonia, Wales. At twenty-one, with dreams larger than his pockets and wider than the Atlantic Ocean, he leaves his mountain dwelling to go and track down the lost tribe of the Madogwys.

MADOG

Legendary superhero Welsh prince who, it has been told, discovered America in 1170. His descendants are thought to be the tribe of Welsh-speaking Native American Madogwys who (possibly) still roam the Great Plains of America.

DAFYDD DDU ERYRI

(Black David of Snowdonia) Great poet, and mentor and teacher to the young John Evans, he introduces Evans to the tale of Madog and to Iolo Morganwg.

IOLO MORGANWG

A literary prankster, revolutionary and Druid. His magnetism pulls Evans into the fast circle of the London Welsh diaspora, from which he is launched to North America to find the lost grail of the Welsh empire.

PETE FOWLER AND THE FELT MISTRESS

A double act who dare to pluck Evans from the quicksand of time and rebuild him for a new age.

VIG VACATION

Present-day travel operator and concert promoter at the arts and entertainment booking agency WheredoUwannago.com in New York.

GWYN 'ALF' WILLIAMS

Popular historian and scholar of Madog and Evans, he once lived on the same street as your host:

GRUFF RHYS

A songwriter and musician, descended from John Evans's maternal uncle, I am searching for the remains of my distant cousin by following his trail through Wales and North America, using the subterfuge of an investigative concert tour. I hope you enjoy the presentation, and thank you for choosing *American Interior*.

ONE

OF THE IMPROBABILITY
THAT
I WOULD EVER ENCOUNTER
A FIRST NATION AMERICAN
SAGEBRUSH RITUAL
IN THE
CANTON DISTRICT OF CARDIFF

(And in which I become a feature of said ritual)

I n 1999 I was asked to write a musical score for a theatre production about the life of the explorer John Evans. I knew his story well, of course, so it seemed only natural that when the Native American and Welsh co-producers were looking for a songwriter, given my connection to him, they approached me.

I turned up late to my first meeting with the theatre company. In a modest brick building in the beautifully scruffy Canton district of Cardiff, Wales, I was unexpectedly initiated into the cast by ritual. I was made to sit on the floor, in a small circle of Native American and Welsh actors, by the veteran theatre director Elfed Lewis, briefed on the significance of the circle in Native American culture, then cleansed by the smoke of burning sagebrush by Carlisle Antonio, one of the long-haired actors.

Using a feather taken from the plumage of Crazy Horse and given to him by the great leader's descendants, Carlisle immersed me in the smoke by fanning the feather up and down and around my body. I felt partly elated but also undeserving of such an accolade. I had the nudging feeling that I was a fraud and that it was all too reminiscent of a scene in that awful Doors biopic by Oliver Stone. I briefly imagined turning into an eagle or wolf or something, and, in the movie adaptation, I will.

Although I had refused to let myself go fully in the ceremony, when I returned home the generosity afforded to me from my cleansing became apparent, and I immediately began to write a 'round', or circular song, for the play. It seemed the principled thing to do. And it got me thinking deeper than ever before about John Evans's strange and unusual journey.

A week later – on another frosty winter's morning – I returned to Canton to play my music to the theatre group. The cast were in tears, however: Elfed Lewis, the bearded director, had collapsed at the previous day's rehearsal and died overnight.

I never did get another opportunity to play them the round, but it goes like this:

Translation: 'Here we are, sailing again, in circular time.'

TWO

THE LIFE OF A MUSICIAN
AND
THE COSMIC OMNIPRESENCE
OF
GWYN A. WILLIAMS

So, as I was saying, I am a songwriter and musician, and I am often called upon to travel around, playing my songs. Seemingly by chance, this touring will occasionally lead to some unexpected opportunity, or bring into my possession something that would have been completely unimaginable in my pre-touring life. For example, a collection of 1970s Turkish and Greek disco 7-inch singles; a pumpkin decorated with a hand-painted American flag in Athens, Georgia, by a member of the Olivia Tremor Control; and a green leather 'Nigeria' fridge magnet from Fela Kuti's Shrine in Lagos. I've also, much to my surprise, acquired a working knowledge of Mexican mezcal production, Italian Socialist libraries, Japanese toilet fittings and the most potent betel nuts in Taipei. I often wonder to myself, 'How did this happen?'

When I first moved to the Welsh capital city of Cardiff at the age of twenty-four to try to make my fortune with the Super Furry

Animals, it was to a ground-floor flat on the Taff Embankment in the Strangetown district, in September, and it rained every day for four months. I had to wear waterproof overalls at all times. It was like living on a ship at sea, although I must admit I have no direct experience of this.

I now live in a Victorian terraced house in the French quarter, on the west side of the River Taff, which divides the city of Cardiff down the middle. I've lived in this house ever since I was thrown out of that nice flat above a bar in the student district, that time just after the referendum.

On this magical litter-strewn strip you can hear Welsh, English, Urdu, Punjabi, Cantonese, Thai, Malay, Romanian, Arabic and Somali – all spoken as first languages. I mostly speak Cat. I share the house with three of them, an older female and her two kittens. They don't have human names yet. It was a casual garden arrangement at first, then a few years ago I let her into the house for the first time. I also have a mountain goat, who lives in the back garden, but he doesn't like to be talked about so much. I am represented by a manager, who works out of an office a couple of blocks away, where the faxes are sent in to invite me on tour. She formerly managed a popular Scottish heavy-metal act that once had a number-one hit in Belgium.

As the whole world is represented in this part of the city, it should have come as no great surprise to me one day when my uncle mentioned that the popular historian Gwyn 'Alf' Williams had once lived on the very same street. In 1979 he published a great book, *Madoc: The Making of a Myth*, which was based on the research he undertook when he fronted a BBC documentary film of the same name, directed by Wil Aron.

At the time, Aron was better known for shooting Welsh-language horror films such as *Gwaed ar y Sêr* ('Blood on the Stars', 1976), in which leading Welsh celebrities were murdered in a variety of crude fashions by an evil kids' choir; and *O'r Ddaear Hen* ('Out of the Ancient Earth', 1981), in which an ancient sacrificial stone turns up in the potato patch of an Anglesey council house, to deadly effect.

Not being taken up by any major cinema distributors, and in the absence back then of a Welsh-language TV channel, *Gwaed ar y Sêr* was screened in villages and school halls the length and breadth of the mountainous country. When my mother took me to watch it as a six-year-old, I had to be carried out, screaming, after Barry John, Wales's most celebrated sporting hero, was torn to shreds by an exploding football. I witnessed *O'r Ddaear Hen* on a school trip at eleven; it gave me nightmares for months, and I was unable to close the curtains at night for years in fear that the Devil himself would jump out from behind the drapery and strangle me, as he had done to others, a running motif in the movie. And indeed, fantastical horror motifs in the form of melting southern sunsets and medieval fanfares pepper Williams's academic overview of the Madog myth.

Significantly for my journey of verification, the book and the film include a detailed chapter or two on John Evans's incredible journey in search of Madog's descendants in America. In a clear and excitable stutter, Williams romanticizes the story and boosts the colour to maximum effect. Following my brush with Crazy Horse's feather, this film became my guide to the life of John Evans, and the fact that the legendary Gwyn A. Williams had lived on my street whilst shooting it seemed an utterly unlikely cosmic coincidence.

Marshal Tito of Yugoslavia had been Williams's hero and political guide, and after learning Italian to write about the communist leader Antonio Gramsci, he documented Welsh history through a series of books framed by the struggles of the working classes, from

THREE

THE HISTORY
OF
IMPERIAL WALES

*Or how Prince Madog (possibly) discovered
America in the twelfth century*

Wales, a rocky peninsular outcrop sticking out of the west of England into the Irish Sea, was the last refuge of the Brythonic 'Welsh' people, who had once roamed throughout the British Isle* but by the sixteenth century had been pummelled remorselessly by the emerging English crown, ever since the Romans had left.

In 1282 Prince Llywelyn (the last monarch of the Cunedda dynasty, which had ruled over a fluid Brythonic proto-Welsh state for a millennium) was killed in an ambush by Edward I's men. According to popular myth, when the Welsh declared that they would never accept an English-speaking ruler, Edward (who was in any case a French-speaking Norman) proclaimed his then-mute baby son (and future Edward II) the Prince of Wales (a sadistic joke, which, whether true or not, remains a tradition of the Windsor

---

* The Brythonic people once occupied the British island as far north as Dunbarton in Scotland. The Welsh, Breton and Cornish languages are for the most part descendants of the Brythonic language.

crown to this day: the heir apparent receives the title of the Welsh principality).

In the fifteenth century Owain Glyndŵr staged a rebellion, crowned himself prince, pledged an allegiance to the French Pope and set up the first Welsh parliament, in the centrally located town of Machynlleth. It was short-lived and Wales fell again, becoming the first colony of the English empire. The Welsh were forbidden from filling any official role, Glyndŵr's planned university towns were scrapped and the new colonial state was administered from Ludlow, a market town located safely over the border in England. Then, in 1536, the Act of Union officially placed Wales under the direct rule of London.

The self-esteem of the Welsh was at an all-time low. The great Cistercian abbeys on the sites of the early Celtic churches, which housed the ancient manuscripts of Welsh civilization, would soon be burned to the ground, and any small glory that could be salvaged from the wreck of old Wales would have seemed like a beacon of hope – a confirmation that this damp, cold, mountainous land had once been a major colonial power; as the American musician Ian Svenonius would say, 'the Portugal of the North'!

It was out of this depressing vacuum that the legend of Madog emerged. From a cynical perspective, Prince Madog was a most useful invention, based on a thirteenth-century romantic saga, 'Madoc', concerning a Welsh seafarer of Viking blood, from the pen of the Flemish bard 'Willem', best known for 'Reynard the Fox'. It was Dr John Dee, a mystic of Welsh descent (and from a republican standpoint, the Goebbels to Queen Elizabeth I's Hitler), who presented Madog as a historical figure – taking liberties with a post-Columbus Welsh take on the Madog story by his contemporary Humphrey Llwyd.

As the great colonial powers of Europe began to cast their greedy nets towards the Americas, Dee realized that if he could prove that the medieval Welsh had already settled there it would give a Brythonic monarch a moral claim to those lands, which were already being snapped up rapidly by the Spanish.

Thus, on 3 October 1580, Madog flapped and stumbled like an ill-prepared penguin into the history books. Dee, having upgraded and rebranded the jurisdiction of the English crown to what he now called the British empire, had prepared a warrant for Elizabeth, along with a map that claimed virtually the whole of North America in her name, on the basis that 'The Lorde Madoc, sonne to Owen Gwynedd, Prince of Northwales, led a colonie and inhabited in Terra Florida or thereabowts.'

'Thereabowts' was audaciously vague of Dee, so as time passed the (possibly imagined) historical narrative of Madog's epic journey was developed into a four-act structure by a succession of sensational propaganda-makers:

ACT ONE

Madog was deemed to be not only one of the sons of the great ruler Owain Gwynedd but also a Viking. (Although Willem wrote about a Celtic man of Viking blood, and Owain Gwynedd did indeed marry the daughter of Dublin's Viking court, there is no historical evidence that Gwynedd ever had a son called Madog. But hey, let's be flexible here.)

ACT TWO

Madog was believed to have left the lands of Gwynedd (the northern powerhouse of old Wales) and sailed to the Americas. Having found a great land of milk and honey, he returned to pick up some more of his compatriots; thirteen boatloads, to be precise. (This figure came into being in a nineteenth-century song by Ceiriog, but why let the prosaic get in the way of quality misinformation?)

ACT THREE

In 1170 Madog was thought to have landed specifically in Mobile Bay, modern-day Alabama, in the Gulf of Mexico – or so claimed John Dee, in his bid to facilitate Francis Drake's sixteenth-century claim for the lands of the emperor of Mexico. (It was plausible that some Nordic, Basque and even Celtic nomads had reached North America via the icebergs of the north much earlier than the late Middle Ages – just ask Leif Ericsson. But Welsh people reaching Alabama? In a coracle? Well, OK, if you insist . . .)

ACT FOUR

Madog then made his way up the Mississippi basin with his tribe of Welsh warriors, finally reaching the upper Missouri River, where his tribe remained, roaming the plains for centuries as a nation of pale-skinned, Welsh-speaking nomads – y Madogwys – who by the eighteenth century had been 'identified' as the Mandan nation.

What a story! The Welsh, although best placed to realize that it might be a complete hoax, loved it. As the centuries passed, and especially when Britain was at war with Spain (which was still in possession of the bulk of colonized North America), yet more texts were written about this unlikely Welsh pioneer.

In the last decade of the eighteenth century a new Wales was emerging. Out of the shackles of centuries of serfdom and subordination to the gentry, the Industrial Revolution was unfolding, in tandem with radical new ideas concerning the freedoms and rights of the oppressed.

A Teutonic Protestant Reformation was used as an excuse to shun the Church of England. The Welsh language, still spoken throughout Wales, was about to enter a period of renaissance as a written language, pioneered by a new elite of exiled and cultured London-based Welsh who now claimed Madog as their own conquistador.

Their imaginations danced to the fantastical prose of one man, a noble savage from the Vale of Glamorgan, a man who dared rescue Wales from a dire Puritan death and who spun its people into a Druidic frenzy. This man was Iolo Morganwg. He promised to travel to the New World to find the Madogwys and bring forth a new age of Welsh empire, and soon the poor farmhand John Evans would be plucked from obscurity to fulfil this impossible task.

Iolo Morganwg was a dangerous, deranged genius, but to begin to understand his utopian ideology we must enter, not a vortex of pulsating ritualistic standing stones, but a franchised coffee shop on a busy shopping street in present-day South Wales. How do you take yours?

FOUR

TIME TRAVEL
AT
COWBRIDGE COFFEE FRANCHISE

C osta Coffee is a particularly drab chain of British coffee shops with a suitably drab coffee colour scheme in their uniform interiors. When the espresso renaissance hit the UK in the 1990s, a slew of chain companies mushroomed out of control around this rainiest of islands, emblazoned with vaguely continental names: Costa, Ritazza, Nero, Pret A Manger. For a people previously accustomed only to milky tea, warm beer and an instant, powdered coffee derivative, the power of an industrial-strength coffee shot was a revelation: workers abandoned their midday pint, pubs closed down and the real bean was embraced like one of the early pagan gods.

Today the British coffee market is considered by analysts to be leaving its infantile period, as the public grow accustomed to the strong coffee shot, undiluted by the traditional full-fat cow's milk. But still, in most cases, in this cold climate the caffè latte is king, and Costa has the milkiest latte since the invention of the café au lait. Of the chains it also has the most sugar-coated pastries and is, indeed, the most popular. I walk into one of its coffee shops on a busy Saturday just before Christmas in Cowbridge, Wales.

A tidy but not overly picturesque market town in the midst of the rich pastures of the Vale of Glamorgan, Cowbridge, due to a number of geographical coincidences – in particular its proximity to the capital city of Cardiff, a multitude of military bases and the M4 motorway corridor – has become the most affluent town in Wales. It wasn't always the case, and this shop was not always a popular coffee emporium, for beyond the jam-filled muffins and the marshmallow-filled babyccinos, the soul of this building belongs to the first contemporary Druid: Iolo Morganwg. It was in the window of this very shop that, at the turn of the nineteenth century, Iolo put up this notice:

EAST INDIA SWEETS

– *Uncontaminated with Human Gore*

My rather flat 'flat white' isn't exactly a magic potion, but pretty soon I have time-travelled back over 200 years and I'm sitting, not in the most banal milk bar in town, but in the cradle of the new Welsh civilization, a radical place where the rights of men, women and bards are universal. Out in the streets the muted clatter of horses' hooves resonates from the muddy, unpaved road and reverberates on the limestone walls of the shop, much as Iolo's baroque seeds of ideas rattled around the minds of his small band of faithful customers.

Iolo Morganwg had opened a bookshop on this site in 1795, but after it failed as a business he turned it into a radical grocery. Unlike the other groceries in town, he refused to stock cheap sugar from the Caribbean, the production of which relied on the labour of slaves. His righteous proto-fair-trade stand shamefully did not resonate with the public, and soon Iolo, by now in his mid fifties, was bankrupt again. Clearly Iolo was not cut out for commerce. His third attempt at maintaining the shop was to turn it into a lending library, which naturally didn't pay the bills either.

Here we have an insight into the interior space that fed the mind of John Evans's mentor, and it would have been in this location that Iolo would have heard of the various hazards that Evans had encountered during his journey. It was from this safe vantage point that Iolo would have followed the extraordinarily chaotic fate of his easily manipulated young pawn.

A truly sad thought, and suddenly the brown world of corporate coffee reappears. Undiminished, I buy a bag of their roasted beans to take home. I toy with the idea that the presence of Iolo in this building hath blessed their contents and given them supernatural powers, undermining the brand's careful, methodical cultivation of a wholesome familial image by secretly empowering those drinkers in the know with supreme skills of time transference, light-speed travel and an unlimited poetic licence.

FIVE

IOLO MORGANWG

*And the gradual unleashing of crass rays of
propaganda and pure fantasy that may ultimately bring
great danger to our friend John Evans*

A stonemason by inherited trade, Iolo appears in the church births register in 1747 as Edward Williams, born in a then-rural cottage in Pennon near Llancarfan, a cottage that remains unchanged, except that today it sits next to the jumbo-jet-certified runway of Cardiff International Airport. From this now-unlikely location, this self-taught artisan was to become the leading light in the revival of late-medieval Welsh literature. He would come to delight a new breed of connoisseurs of the Welsh language with his unparalleled crate-digging skills, unearthing text after lost text of ancient literature from the likes of Dafydd Ap Gwilym, a romantic balladeer regarded as the Welsh Chaucer.

It became apparent to early-twentieth-century academics that this was down to Morganwg's skill as a forger, and that he had simply written extraordinarily complex works in the style of the leading bards to the point of improving on the work of the originals. But this is only the half of it.

Many of his countless written words were committed to paper inside the walls of Cardiff prison, as his vocation certainly didn't fill his pockets with any cash; he walked around Wales like a possessed, mystic tramp, gathering reams of documents, folk tales and *cywyddau* (poems) to add to his huge collection of prose, ever expanding not only his knowledge but also his mounting debts to the taxman. Increasingly disparate periods as a stonemason kept the food on his growing family's table, between bouts of bankruptcy.

At the turn of the 1790s it dawned on him that to become a fully professional writer he needed to expand his horizons, so he moved to London, leaving his wife, Margaret, and children behind in the Vale.

In his new situation he played up his folksy image and dazzled the new class of London-based 'Gwyneddigion' revivalists with his knowledge and zeal for everything Welsh. He had some success in networking in his new environment, and the subscribers to his first English publication, *Poems, Lyric and Pastoral* (two volumes, 1792–4), included both George Washington and William Penn. This didn't blunt his political purpose, however, and his preface to *The Myvyrian Archaeology of Wales* (the first compendium of Welsh literature through the ages) is considered the first text of modern-day Welsh separatism.

We must remember that, in the wake of the American Revolution and its French counterpart, these were heady days. Anything was possible. Existing truths were there to be destroyed. There was a brief window of opportunity in the early 1790s when even the monarchy could be challenged by the Jacobin spirit of the age. Whole cultures lay waiting for reinvention.

In the days leading up to John Evans's departure for a new world, anti-slavery activist Morgan John Rhys, fresh from witnessing the revolution in Paris, published the first Welsh-language dissident magazine, known simply as *Cylchgrawn* (Welsh for 'magazine'). In

1792 Mary Wollstonecraft published her *Vindication of the Rights of Woman*. It was a radical age, and in the middle of it all Iolo fancifully provided a map for his fellow countrymen that connected the dots between a progressive egalitarian future and a past firmly rooted in the ancient Druidic pastimes of the Welsh.

Today, from the summit of Primrose Hill in London, you can witness the towering crystalline panorama of the twenty-first-century London skyline. Study the ground beneath your feet, however, and you will notice a slate plaque. It commemorates the first ritual of the modern-day Welsh Druidic order 'Gorsedd y Beirdd' – the Order of the Bards. 'Revived' by Iolo Morganwg and based (according to him) on documentation he had acquired concerning the old rites of the Brythonic Druids, it was in reality a mish-mashed concoction of his love of Stonehenge and the imagined rites of the Neolithic stone circles, with a dash of the freemasonic symbolism that was all the rage at the time. This was typical of Iolo the asthmatic's laudanum-laced imagination (he was a lifelong addict).*

We can only speculate about whether John Evans was there on the momentous occasion of this spectacle, but it seems reasonable to assume that half the clientele of the Bull's Head tavern in Walbrook and the Prince of Wales coffee house on Conduit Street, both of which he frequented, were participating on the day. It could have served as a great send-off for this learned young man, who by this point was aching to set sail to America.

The Gorsedd y Beirdd was initially a modest affair, and Iolo was not to know that the Welsh would completely accept his idiosyncratic fabrication as a genuine tradition bequeathed to them by the Druids

---

* The main active ingredient of laudanum was opium, but this was partially diluted with a lovely infusion of alcohol, saffron, nutmeg and sugar.

of yore. Indeed, today, in the twenty-first century, every August his 500-strong order of Druids, complete with robes, swords and, bizarrely, colourful wellington boots, perform three bardic rituals during an action-packed Eisteddfod* week, in front of a seated audience of 2,000 people, broadcast live on TV to thousands more. Stone circles have been erected in every town to facilitate past and potential visits by the 'Gorsedd', and the Druidic order has become a de facto order of merit for the stateless Welsh and includes rugby players, academics and soap actors in blue, white or green robes, and, in the starry firmament, wearing golden robes, the poets.

But let us now return to 1792 and the first rite on Primrose Hill. Facing south-east we see the smoky spires of central London, but at the summit of the hill, Iolo Morganwg, the Archdruid, is handing out awards of medals to the best poets. Here, to our right, is a young man with an inquisitive face: John Evans.

* The annual festival of Welsh-language culture.

SIX

IEUAN AB IFAN:
THE EARLY YEARS

Or the first transformation of John Evans
(one of his many Bowie-style reinventions)

John Evans was born on 14 April 1770 at Gwredog Uchaf, a smallholding perched on a damp slope outside Waunfawr, during the white heat of a particularly Welsh form of Methodist Reformation. His grandfather, Ifan Dafydd (not to be confused with the dubstep producer of the same name), of whom I am a direct descendant, was a learned preacher of some repute, as was his father, Thomas Evans, who was so popular that he could go on paid preaching tours to South Wales that lasted six weeks. Evan Evans, John's younger brother by three years, would himself follow in their footsteps, but John, though immersed in Methodism, developed interests that would propel him in another direction entirely.

It seems likely that he formed a close bond with his young teacher Dafydd Ddu Eryri (Black David of Snowdonia), a promising local poet who eventually rose to national attention. Although John Evans's informal education would have been piecemeal, he had an intellectual rigour forged by the verbal acrobatics performed at Methodist gatherings, his theological discussions with his father and brother, and, more importantly perhaps, his friendship with Dafydd Ddu Eryri, who would have introduced John to the cultural discussions of the day.

The hot topic, of course, was Madog. The lost tribe of the Madog-wys was the theme of a famous Dafydd Ddu Eryri poem that won him a prize at the Llanrwst Eisteddfod of 1790. Dafydd fantasized about reaching these estranged Welsh and converting them to the Methodist cause. The London Welsh patrons of culture weren't so keen on the stifling intensity of Calvinism, which sought to destroy the folk trad-itions, especially in music, but were swayed enough by the charm of Dafydd's recital and its powerful animation of the lost tribe.

Dafydd was a pillar of his community, and although from humble beginnings he became important as a teacher, as the Welsh-language Bible boom produced a new level of literacy amongst the peasant and working classes, a literacy now channelled through a network of independent schools run by the new ideologues. He found an eager pupil eleven years his junior in the restless Evans and was much loved by all and sundry.*

The rejection of the Church of England must be seen in a political dimension. Waunfawr was a monolingual Welsh-speaking valley, but when the parish church officials recorded births and deaths they tweaked the Welsh-language names of their parishioners out of exist-ence. In the first of many transformations, Ieuan ab Ifan became John Evans, and for the people of his valley, joining a supplementary reli-gious grouping, as they did at their inaugural Methodist congregation in 1746, would have been an intuitive way of expressing their distinct identity as Welsh people.

A myriad of independent denominations of varying degrees of

---

* Curiously, Dafydd was to drown at the then-grand age of sixty-one, his body found face down in the River Cegin after a stormy winter's night.

solemnity would begin the process of breaking away from the colonially administered Church, led initially by charismatic messianic figures such as Hywel Harris, who never smiled and would whip his young Emo-like audience into a frenzied yet solemn devotion to piety, until he was thrown out of his own Methodist movement after a sex scandal involving 'Madam' Sidney Griffith.* He then retired to the 'Trefeca Family' commune he had established in rural Wales, where his followers grew vegetables and called him 'Father'.†

The rebel denominations would meet at informal locations – in each other's houses or even in caves – but eventually their familiar box-like stone chapels mushroomed across Wales, through every city and mountain hamlet, including Waunfawr. Today Waunfawr is a friendly village that fills the bottom of a deep valley, flanked by an unusual, elephant-shaped mountain (it's true, it really looks like an elephant) bearing the prosaic name locally of Mynydd Eliffant (*mynydd* = mountain) but which the Ordnance Survey map identifies as Mynydd Mawr (Big Mountain). In Evans's day the valley housed a disparate collection of rural dwellings in small hillside clusters, and the main trade of the area, which Evans too would have participated in, was producing and weaving wool into cord for the local mill at Betws Garmon. Clothes were made for the copper miners of Nantlle

* Harris was a frequent visitor to Hafod y Rhug, Evans's maternal grandfather Ifan Dafydd's home.

† By the twentieth century most Welsh people had disowned the Church of England and flocked to the independent churches, which became de facto schools and cultural centres for the working classes, saving the Welsh language's existence in the process. In addition, the fact that the Church had imposed only English bishops on Welsh cathedrals for the last 150 years caused the rank and file finally to rebel, and the Anglican Church in Wales, battling for survival, eventually separated from the Church of England in 1920.

and the workers at the small slate quarries that were scattered around the mountains.

At the heart of the present-day village lies an extraordinary institution called Antur Waunfawr (Waunfawr Venture). A progressive community-based cooperative that employs many people and also finds work in the community for people with disabilities, it provides green recycling services for an area that spans far beyond the locality. Its ethos is that everyone should make their utmost contribution to society, and that everyone in society should be allowed to play their part, no matter what their circumstances. Within its headquarters, there is a one-room John Evans exhibition where local people can get to know the John Evans story and perhaps be inspired to set out on an adventure of their own. You can even sit in Dafydd Ddu Eryri's original carved wooden chair.

My friend Haydn ended up working here after his American soccer adventure, and, being an active and useful participant in society, knows practically everyone in the valley. He's a coach at youth level for the magnificent three-time Welsh Premier League champions Bangor City Football Club. He's also a coach of the local Waunfawr soccer team, where he teaches the children of the present occupiers of Gwredog Uchaf, John Evans's birthplace.

On an overcast, cold and windy day, I jump into the passenger seat of Haydn's blue car at Antur Waunfawr and we head for the house where John Evans was born. We are greeted by a burly Lancastrian called John Roughly, who met his North Walian wife Gail in the Falkland Islands, where they were both stationed in the health service, after the Malvinas war.

Both still employed in healthcare at the local hospital, they are extremely welcoming and give us a candid view of their home. The living room is pretty much how it would have been in Evans's day, except for the flat-screen TV. The small upstairs bedroom where Evans was born even bears a felt-tipped plaque with the words 'Jack's Room', made by their son. They aren't native Welsh speakers, but their children, having been educated at the local school in Waunfawr, are fluent, in what is still an overwhelmingly Welsh-speaking area.

The family are, in a very matter-of-fact way, in tune with the supernatural and claim the house is haunted by a polite enough milk-maid. The house was built into the hillside in 1750 and looks down the mountain to the colossal Caernarfon Castle, four miles away. They are currently building an extension, and they mention that they would like to include some stones from Evans's place of burial, wher-ever that may be, in its construction.

John Evans's mother, Ann, died in 1777 when he was young, probably during the birth of his sister Jane. Although Gwredog Uchaf is hardly a big house, when John was seven years old his father moved the family across to the east side of the valley to a yet smaller hillside cottage at Hafod Olau, one of a group of one-storey dwellings up on the common land of the mountain.

Driving up this sharp elevation of a thousand feet to Hafod Olau is a revelation for a John Evans enthusiast. Facing west, the house looks out over the dark waves of the Irish Sea, with all the mysterious possibilities of distant lands. When Evans first heard of the Madogwys,

the lost Welsh-descended tribe and the theme of Dafydd's famous recital, it's no wonder that he felt compelled to go and find them, having spent most of his life looking out to the oceans from his towering vantage point in the clouds.

When John visited the 1790 Eisteddfod, most probably with Dafydd Ddu Eryri, it's likely that he encountered Iolo Morganwg for the first time and was witness to a fiery sermon in which Iolo called for the Americans, in light of Madog's legacy, to present the Welsh with their own tract of land in the new country of the free, so that the Welsh could leave their condemned royalist homeland.

In 1791, his mind no doubt at bursting point with the promise of a world beyond his drizzle-bound mountain, John Evans moved to London, England, with seemingly little preparation. It would have taken him weeks to make the journey on foot. His arrival not only coincided with a time of war (once again) between the British and Spanish, but also with the publication of a new book on Madog, the latest in a long line of dodgy dossiers written since Dee's original effort. This one, which brought the subject to fever pitch, was written by John Williams and had the best title yet:

An Enquiry into the Truth of the Tradition, Concerning the Discovery of America, by Prince Madog ab Owen Gwynedd, about the Year, 1170

In its wake, when Iolo Morganwg announced in London during a true fantasist's fit of bravado that he was looking for able-bodied assistants to join him in his quest to reach the Madogwys tribe, there was only one volunteer: John Evans.

What did the 21-year-old orphan have to lose? With his father newly deceased and his younger siblings of a mature age, to the dismay of his pious brethren (who were worried that he was driven by vanity and greed) he was now resident in London, having joined the pulsating heart of the freewheeling Welsh literary movement, but, unlike some of his hosts, with very little means and only an occasional roof over his head. Psychiatrist Ceri Evans believes that the trauma of losing his mother at such a young age could have had a profound effect on the chemical make-up of Evans's brain, making him far more susceptible to risk-taking. And hanging out with Iolo was a risky business.

It was just as well that Evans was single-minded in the extreme. Whimsical Iolo, it soon transpired, although committed to a military fitness regime in preparation for the cross-continental adventure, had a family of dependants and, in truth, had no real intention of going: soon enough he was back in the (future coffee) shop in Cowbridge.

It's probable that Iolo fully understood the precarious nature of the Madog story, as he was partly responsible for fanning its flames, but, ever the optimist, he was unable to resist the political and romantic implications of Madog as a genuine historical figure. In any case, Evans alone now had to lead the charge (and raise the money) for this grand, possibly deluded, expedition to the mysterious lands of the White Padoucas.

Iolo's motto for his new bardic order of Druids was '*Y Gwir yn erbyn y Byd*' ('The Truth against the World'). Iolo was undoubtedly a genius, but he was also a fraud of the highest order. Evans, however, took this motto to heart. Like the best investigative journalists, albeit with a soft spot for the fantastical, he would strive to achieve his goal regardless of worldly restrictions and rational thought processes and was willing to travel to the extremities of the known world to do so. But first he needed to appeal to the glittering radical minds of London for the funding of his one-man expedition.

SEVEN

HARNESSING THE BULL'S HEAD

And what does Evans look like, anyway?

The gaps in knowledge and the mysteries surrounding John Evans are more numerous than the facts. R. Gwynn Davies, a prominent lawyer who hailed, like Evans, from Waunfawr, remarked in a twentieth-century lecture on his hero that he would never have depended on him as a witness in a court of law, as from what we can gather from Evans's correspondence and the observations of his contemporaries, he is an unreliable narrator, often given to exaggeration.

One startling fact for the children of the age of digital surveillance is that there are no known images of Evans in existence. As portraits were the curiosities of the privileged classes, we can only speculate about his physical appearance. He might have had the classical build of the prehistoric Welsh mountains: the short stature and dark Iberian looks of the Beaker people. But he was born only four miles from the highway of the oceans and the booming port of Caernarfon on the Irish Sea, so he could have had Nordic, Berber or Asian features. Was his hair red, blond, black, curly, bobbed, crew-cut? Was he short, tall, wide, lanky, three-fingered or knock-kneed? Did he have sticky-out ears, webbed feet or an aristocratic nose? How could we ever know?

Pondering this question one morning whilst drinking a coffee brewed from the beans I picked up from Iolo's old shop, I stumble upon the idea that I should try to rebuild John Evans from scratch to make him a tangible figure for people to imagine. Just as it seems like a leap today to feel empathy for the victims of famine or natural disaster without video news footage, it often seems truly hard for people to root for someone without some visual information. In the case of John Evans, it needn't be a showy, Steve Austin-style bionic man, or even a Power Ranger-like superhero; a low-tech avatar will do the job: just a modest means of reintroducing this forgotten explorer to the world. I'm not too sure that Evans would concur with my idea, but I like to think Iolo would approve.

I get to work immediately. Consumed in a frenzy of enthusiasm, I print out a series of illustrative archetypes: family mugshots, promo photos and paintings of prominent personalities from Waunfawr, along with images of the typical male fashions of the late eighteenth century. I stick them up on the wall, where they resemble the pinboard at a crime investigation unit, then I quickly rethink the situation, roll them up into a cardboard tube, run out of the house to Cardiff Central Station and head to London on the 10.25 train.

At Liverpool Street Station I stumble from the Tube, carrying my tube, and head into the wind to Bethnal Green Road. I'm on my way to see a friend by the name of Pete Fowler, who is an illustrator, a specialist of the unimaginable. If anyone can visualize our protagonist with any degree of flair, it's Pete. His studio is perched on the first floor of a seemingly dilapidated factory building.

We are only a mile or so from the site of the Bull's Head tavern, on a street called Walbrook, near the Bank of England, where the London Welsh societies the Gwyneddigion and the Caredogion would meet every Monday to discuss politics, poetry and Madog under the grizzly gaze of the Welsh proprietor, Evan Williams. Having arrived in London in 1791, Evans would have spent a lot of his time here, trying to raise cash for his expedition, singing the songs of home and stumbling back to his lodgings (when he had any), drunk on new ideas.

In London, Evans was exposed to many new things. We know that, along with his contemporaries Iolo Morganwg and Morgan John Rhys, he flirted with freemasonry, and even though we might presume that his religious background would have precluded him from anything beyond the raging London coffee boom, rumours of alcoholism have always dogged his story. He was just a youngster burning with the incandescent flame of curiosity, and it's possible he had to adopt a new flexibility to cope with his ever-changing environment. Even Morgan John Rhys, a fully fledged preacher, was, according to his journals, a connoisseur of the occasional fine alcoholic drink, so we can speculate that Evans could have had the odd tipple by the time he left the metropolis.

From his correspondence with his brother, we know that he was homeless for a long time when he arrived in the city. But by 1792 he was lodging with fellow Welsh exiles Hugh Beauchamp and Huw Roberts. Indeed, when Iolo's grand plans to explore the West collapsed, it was Roberts who lent Evans £20 in late August 1792 for an American crossing. Evans apparently had an honest face, one that he would use again and again to earn the trust of the people he encountered, however unlikely it was that he would ever see them again, let alone repay a loan. In fact, once he was in America, Evans did everything he could to elude repaying his former friend, setting a pattern that would be characteristic throughout his journey.

Just as Evans had to come to London to start his adventure, I have now followed in his footsteps in an attempt to get to know him a little better. I'm not sure how far I'm willing to travel to satisfy my curiosity, so I decide to play it by ear and let Iolo's beans do the rest. I walk upstairs to Pete's studio, empty the rolled-up contents of my tube on to his desk, and together we embark upon our journey: to conjure up John Evans from our imaginations and the footnotes of history, in order to transform him into a twenty-first-century avatar.

EIGHT

SANS CULOTTES?

The rise of the thin grey duke

We recreate my crime-solving wall of mugshots in Pete's London studio and study the evidence. The printed images include Dafydd Iwan, a prominent Welsh-language protest balladeer; a painting of Evans's poet friend Dafydd Ddu Eryri; snapshots of members of my family, my paternal grandmother in particular; and a couple of promo shots of the sensational 1990s Waunfawr rock band Beganifs.

It's unfair to assume that a pious farmhand and occasional weaver from the mountains would be dressed in the latest fashions of the London dandy, so we select clothes from the 1770s to the 1790s.

We wonder whether he would have worn breeches. 'Culottes' were considered the trouser uniform of the bourgeoisie by the 'Sans Culottes' – the ground warriors of the French Revolution, who preferred the long trousers of the peasant working class – but although Evans's character seems to fit in this revolutionary realm, he was also an idiosyncratic kind of guy, so we decide that breeches will work for our maverick Jacobin Methodist after all. Buckled shoes, a ruffled white shirt, a military-grade felt coat and what we would consider today as a pirate-style hat top him off.

But, what of the face? How can we recreate a face that is both charismatic and 'honest'?

Pete takes the pen. Known primarily as a Monsterist, in recent years his oeuvre has included the sea, sailors and bearded sonic adventurers playing synthesizers on boats – probably a legacy of his epiphanic stint as a boat builder on the Scilly Isles in his formative early twenties. He was born and raised in Cardiff, however, and comes from a lineage of heroic truck-driving fuel protestors who are in turn, arguably, the political descendants of the radical Rebecca rioters of 1839.* His uncle

* The Rebecca Riots, the world's first successful cross-dressing insurgency/publicity stunt, rid Wales of tolled roads in the nineteenth century.

is rumoured to have blockaded the whole of Milford Haven docks by lorry in the early zeros – and as Milford Haven is one of the biggest natural harbours in Europe, this is no idle boast.

So I have a strong sense that as an appreciator of outlaws and both sonic and seafaring exploration, it is only Pete who has the intuition to rescue John Evans's honest face from the depths of the ages.

Indeed, only an Earth yard from my eyes, Evans explodes into life in a riot of permanent markers on Perspex. His thin, crazed face betrays an element of cubism that reveals perfectly the known facets of his personality, yet he radiates a warmth and innocence that gives credence to his charming reputation.

Though I may not have looked upon the face of God, I have now seen the face of John Evans.

NINE

THE FELT MISTRESS

And the chance of a second lifetime

We enlist another Evans – Louise, who hails, like our hero John, from North Wales – to build a three-dimensional version of the man, and only a couple of weeks later a large coffin-shaped cardboard box arrives by Special Delivery at my front door. I carefully use a Stanley knife to cut open the package, and from a blizzard of shredded newspaper I pull out a three-foot-tall adventurer made from grey felt, complete with colonial and Native American accessories.

In a bid to pinpoint particular traits of John Evans's personality, I look through a book of astrology that includes the Chinese zodiac. As he was born on 14 April 1770, he was an Aries and his Chinese year was the Year of the Tiger. I place the felt John on his belly along the sofa. In his back, under the ruffled shirt, there is a small compartment where Anna Loggins, a synthesizer-maker and a friend of mine, has inserted a simple robotic personality function. I open the sliding lid, insert two AA batteries, close it firmly, then scroll through a simple wheel of characteristics on the lid of the compartment, which Loggins has prepared. Consulting the astrology book, I press a blue 'Enter' button on the wheel each time I see a character trait that corresponds with John's. Traits relating to the Aries Tiger include:

PASSION + SPONTANEITY + COURAGE + DRIVE +

SUPERIORITY + OSTENTATION + BRAVERY + INTENSITY +

RESILIENCE + MAGNETISM + AFFABILITY + NAIVETY +

SWAGGER + EXCESS + INTEMPERANCE + TALENT +

GOOD LUCK + AUTHORITY + BENEVOLENCE + ENTERPRISE +

ITINERANCY + REBELLION + DISOBEDIENCE + OBSTINACY

As each trait appears in a small LED window on the robotic personality function, it makes a beep and flashes twice within the red figure-eight structures of the digital numerology. It's hardly cutting-edge robotics, but I think we've got the basics covered.

I sit him down on the sofa, switch on the rolling TV news so he can catch up with what's going on, and head to the kitchen to brew up some of Iolo's beans, tossing a piece of toast to the kittens as I pass them at the bottom of the stairs, in the hope that it will distract them from scratching their claws on our weary adventurer.

I throw some carrot peelings through the window to the goat in the back garden and pour the boiling water over the fine grains of the beans, then take in two lungfuls of aroma. I have a proposition for my new felt friend, and it must be communicated with the utmost sensitivity.

As I pour the treacle-coloured coffee into one of my finest china cups and take a deep gulp, I mull over my momentous decision to offer John the chance of a second lifetime: I will return him to the Americas, and in exchange he will help me discover what happened to him on his original visit; just by being a visual manifestation of his former self, he will make his history plausible for the people we encounter. We will play concerts together, revisit his old haunts and, if we're lucky, maybe we'll find his place of burial. I cut two pieces of lemon drizzle cake, put them on plates and return to the living room with the hot proposal.

Still unaccustomed to speech in his new guise, he nevertheless seems into the idea; at least, he definitely isn't perturbed by the prospect. Instead he maintains his stoic glare through the window, where some of the inhabitants of contemporary Wales play cricket on the street and the Millennium Stadium glistens like an outsized mother ship above the rooftops.

In a musical age where the touring musician can feel like the puppet of consumer forces, and where cities have been renamed *markets* and entire countries downgraded to *territories*, the trajectory of the artist has been blown somewhat off course. My plan is to re-inject purpose into the headless-chicken act of international concert-touring, and to inspire a new era of purposeful touring itineraries. In short, to swing a laminated Access All Areas pass to discovery on the fluorescent lanyard of exploration. As moments in what I call an investigative concert tour, the locations of my shows should be chosen for their significance in the history of John Evans's life, as opposed to their potential 'market power'; and the location of my very last show should be determined by the discovery (or not) of his lost grave. This is my pledge, even if it means, on occasion, playing a set of songs to wild animals in the uninhabited wilderness.

I set up my Korean palmtop computer and immediately start work on the logistics. I phone an arts and entertainment booking agent in New York who was recommended to me by a neighbour, Colin, a former circus performer. The agency is called, worryingly,

WheredoUwannago.com. And its digi flyer commands me to phone it at 0800-WheredoUwannago.

'Hello, Vig speaking, *where* do you wanna go?' is Vig Vacation's taped opening gambit.

'Yes, Vig . . . Hello . . . Baltimore – we'd like to start a tour in Baltimore, please,' I reply, catching my breath whilst trying to remember the key cities of John's long-ago journey.

'Philly; Cincinnati; Louisville, Kentucky –'

'Pittsburgh,' interjects John decisively. 'We'll need to go to Pittsburgh.'

I'm shocked. These are the first words I've heard him utter.

'And Pittsburgh, Vig. We must go to Pittsburgh,' I say, a disturbed expression on my face.

I give him a brief synopsis of John's previous life.

'Oh, inneresting!' enthuses the real Vig. 'I can maybe get you a show at the 4 Bears Casino, North Dakota?' he continues, finishing the 'Dakota' on a high note. 'This is a really neat project. I think we can get a lot of interest from colleges, art centres, stuff like that too.'

He's taking me seriously, which means that this might actually happen. I am elated. John remains stoic.

I just need to let my manager, record company, friends and family know what I'm planning. They're going to kill me, but I call them up regardless.

'That's too long, too crazy, too risky, too not-financially-viable,' says my manager.

'Gruff, that route is brutal. You can't possibly be serious,' says Anna Loggins.

'Jesus, some of those towns don't even exist any more,' says my brother.

'There just aren't enough major markets in the Dakotas,' says my record company when I ask them to pay for the trip.

'I just don't see why you're taking this thing on with that . . . muppet,' says my cat.

'What about us?' ask the kittens.

'Please don't go,' bleats the goat.

ACT TWO, PART ONE

ON THE TRAIL OF JOHN EVANS

A LONG LANE THAT HAS MORE TURNING

PRINCIPAL CHARACTERS

DR SAMUEL JONES

An eighteenth-century Welshman and Baptist pastor living in Philadelphia and the unofficial gatekeeper to the Welsh American diaspora.

MORGAN JOHN RHYS

An anti-slavery campaigner and the founder of the ghost village of Beula. Rhys alerts General Mackay to Evans's project.

BRIGADIER GENERAL JAMES WILKINSON

US general and Spanish double agent who guides Evans to the lands of New Spain.

DINAH MARTIN

'A woman of rare culture and learning', Martin saves Evans's life.

JUDGE GEORGE TURNER

The US judge for the North-west Territory of the River Ohio, based in Kaskaskia, he is Evans's advocate, gets him out of jail and recommends him to the St Louis establishment.

CAROLYN GILMAN

Present-day historian and archaeologist, living in St Louis.

LETTER OF INTRODUCTION
CONCERNING JOHN EVANS,
FROM
IOLO MORGANWG
TO
J. PRITCHARD,
PRINTER AND BOOKSELLER,
PHILADELPHIA

London, August 15th, 1792

Sir

Perhaps you will be able to recollect that when you was last year in London, I waited on you with a Mr Wm Owen, when I showed you a little pamphlet by a Dr J. Williams on the discovery of America by Madog Ap Owain Gwynedd. You told me Sir that you was acquainted with Dr Samuel Jones, who, it seems, knows something of a Tribe of Welsh Indians. The Bearer hereof Mr John Evans is a young Gentleman of Wales, and his chief reason for coming to America is with the view, which most people here think laudable, of making what enquiries he possibly can about these people. Mr Evans is of a very respectable family in Wales, and has always been distinguished for his uncommonly good morals and conduct, he comes not on this intention as an agent or emissary of any political party. Government has not yet been made acquainted with this affair, in which several in Wales are now engaging themselves. I am one of these, and it is our intention to wait some of us on Mr Penkeny your Ambassador to this Country as soon as we can prepare a proper account to lay before him, of the motives of our intended expedition. [W]*e mean to solicit the* [illegible] *sanction of the American States, for our little party are of those who were originally in the opinion of our government rebelliously partial to the Americans, and in America we intend to end our days – Mr Evans would, as well as all his friends here, esteem it a favour if you could give him any of that information that he is so desirous of obtaining, i.e., relating the Welsh Indians, and would be glad to wait on Dr Samuel Jones.*

I am, Sir, your most humble servant

Edward Williams
[Iolo Morganwg]

ONE

BALTIMORE BY BOAT

I t's a rough, seven-week crossing from the flooded mudflats of Tiger Bay, Cardiff, to Baltimore Harbor, the pretty waterfront on which, ironically, the redevelopment of the rebranded Cardiff Bay was modelled in the Conservative 1980s, when Thatcher ran Wales into the ground in time-honoured colonial fashion. Against all odds, my French friend Benoît manages to get the tug that usually carries commuters up and down the River Taff on to the open sea, through the thinnest of locks, and skilfully, as promised, sails it to America. I'm the sickest I've ever been, but John remains calm throughout and is my rock.

John's journey in his previous life was hellish. He borrowed enough money to get him a steerage-class ticket – the worst of the worst class – and landed in Baltimore on 10 October 1792 with little cargo or goods apart from a letter of introduction to Samuel Jones given to him by the esteemed minister from Bala, Thomas Charles, and another from Iolo to a Philadelphia bookseller. Jones was a member of a hugely influential Welsh diaspora based in the temporary capital city of Philadelphia. A Baptist pastor who lived in the Lower Dublin area, he served as an unofficial consul to the stream of curious religious radicals pouring out of Wales to the revolutionary land. The letters from his archive provide an illuminating insight into the rise of a distinctly Welsh revolutionary spirit.

Though some guess at Liverpool as his point of departure, we can speculate that Evans left directly from London, as it seems he never returned to Waunfawr and didn't let his siblings know of his quest to find the Madogwys until after his arrival in America. Maybe he was scared of being talked out of it or just didn't care. In any case he sold it to his brother and local minister in Caernarfon as a missionary campaign – as he also did to the Baptists he would now meet on the East Coast.

After arriving in Baltimore, we can assume Evans would have rested for a few days. He then walked to Philadelphia, and, in his letters to his brother Evan, he describes a 300-mile journey. If we presume that he didn't take an insane detour, this gives us a good indication of the degree of exaggeration that this man indulged in, as the cities are in reality only a hundred miles apart. By 10 November, however, Evans was back in Baltimore, having refused to listen to the advice of Jones and others that he should return home immediately and that his proposed journey to the mysterious American interior was far too dangerous to contemplate.

Upon returning to Baltimore, he wrote to Jones that he had found work at 'one of the finest wholesalers in town where I have the opportunity of learning Surveying'. This was a hugely significant step for Evans, as it would prepare him for the journey ahead. 'I have a firm resolution to make on a attempt next spring . . . my anxiety for the discovery increases more every day,' he adds.

He then quotes from a beautiful Eisteddfod-winning Welsh poem by Dafydd 'Black David' Ddu Eryri concerning the Madogwys, the tribe descended from Madog, which he hopes to discover and convert to Jesus:

Taened goleu tywyniaid gwiwlon
I'r gorllewinol gyrau llawnion,
Gwawr o ddiwygiad gywir ddigon
Draw I Fadawgwys – drefedigion.

[May the beautiful lilting light spread
To fill every corner of the west.
A new dawn for a sincere reformation
Will come to the citizens of the Madogwys.]

He mentions that he has had this printed up as a pamphlet at the expense of Dr Jones himself, presumably to raise money for the journey within the Welsh community (and that he'll pay him back soon). All this comes before a rather unexpected confession – 'My conscience says I must be a Baptist' – after which Evans concludes, 'If you hear anything of Welsh Indians I should be exceedingly glad to hear from you.'

That he was willing to become a Baptist is a shocking statement and reveals to what degree he was prepared to adapt to any given situation. Having been in the United States for only one month, he was about to turn his back on the Methodism practised by three generations of his family. Even in the very late twentieth century in Wales, until the chapels of different denominations began to merge and religion itself began to disintegrate, changing one's denomination was not something that was done lightly. He may have concluded that he was unlikely to return home, and that he now had to play by different rules.

His conversion clearly marked him out as a pragmatist and a social chameleon: he was an obsessed man, driven to achieve his goal, the discovery of the Madogwys, by any means, and at this point he was relying on one of the few assets he had: his charisma.

SOUNDCHECK AT THE GOLDEN WEST CAFÉ

It's unclear what John the Avatar's role will be in the shows I've arranged through WheredoUwannago.com. During the seven-week crossing, before reaching the relative calm of Chesapeake Bay through the Atlantic fog, we had only three smooth days at sea and the question never really came up. Rehearsals were out of the question. I set up some equipment at Baltimore's Golden West Café and check the microphones are working. I have a little screen and slide projector I plan to make use of in the shows – a soft-PowerPoint presentation – and I'm trying to focus the lens when a young woman, who's popped in to buy a ticket for the show, interrupts me.

She's brought me a book, written by her father: an encyclopedia of Welsh chapels in America entitled *Songs of Praises*. Samuel Jones's Lower Dublin chapel stares at me from the back cover. I can take John there tomorrow!

To celebrate, I take my new friend out for an iced coffee at the Daily Grind down the road. She's called Liz Williams and is in college nearby, although she hails originally from Utica, a super-Welsh town in upstate New York. It's boiling hot, over a hundred degrees, so we go and sit by the harbour shore at Fells Point, under the shade of a tree.

Liz is worrying about the futility of maintaining Welsh traditions as a sixth-generation settler who grew up not only observing St David's Day but also using the odd Welsh-language word in conversation.

'Who am I? Why should I even care?' she asks.

Our conversation turns to the fluidity of the whole notion of identity, and we resolve that one aspect of belonging is about community and how people help one another cope with life through communal living – not in the 1968 Bavarian Amon Düül II commune sense, but through small actions, such as bringing each other books that will help us reach our next destination. Which, in my case, is a concert. We return to the café – a vegetarian bar and restaurant where the audience sit at tables facing the stage. It's a Saturday night and it's beginning to fill up with people. Liz combs back her long brown hair with her fingers, gives John a hug goodbye and goes to sit at a table with friends.

I imagine that in 1972, down the road in Washington, DC, it was in this type of music-café scenario that Gram Parsons first set eyes on Emmylou Harris, although the chances of a major music legend stopping by tonight to watch a bearded musician and his three-foot-high felt friend play a repertoire of Welsh-language songs seems highly unlikely.

It's documented that on Christmas Day 1792 in Baltimore, John Evans sang a Dafydd Ddu Eryri song, 'Rywbeth Arall i'w Wneuthur', to a small congregation of Welsh exiles (six people). The song's rather nonchalant title translates as 'Something Else to Do', and it's been my ambition for a while now to sing this song in Baltimore. It will really help turn the show into an Event.

I trawl through my black bag for a photocopy of the song's lyrics. T-shirts, pens and raincoats all come flying out, and eventually I find the song. It's still boiling hot and there's no working air-conditioning system in the building, plus I'm in pain: the lack of fresh water to brush my teeth on the transatlantic boat journey has ruined them, and one in particular aches like it's being continually struck by a large wooden mallet. Regardless, I adjust my shirt, grab hold of John by the neck and head to the stage.

I sing Dafydd's lyrics unaccompanied, then try out a new song about my distant cousin and how, apart from a couple of letters early on in his journey to his brother Evan and to Iolo Morganwg, he didn't write home, transposing it to the age of the email. It goes by the name of '100 Unread Messages':

You landed in America
One fine October day,
Sailing into Baltimore,
Everything's OK.

New buttons on your jacket,
Shining like they're brand-new dimes,
Glistening in the sunlight,
Blistering my eyes.

When you said that you loved me,
I knew it wasn't true.
I've one hundred unread messages,
But not a single note from you . . .

TWO

PHILADELPHIA ARRIVAL

The Count enters the Mausoleum

With:

Songs of Praises
Welsh-Rooted Churches Beyond Britain
by
Jay G. Williams III

on my lap, we head up Interstate 95 in our silver hired wheels towards Philadelphia. I want to take John back to the old Pennepack Baptist Church in Lower Dublin. The book takes us right to the spot.

It's Sunday lunchtime and the church meeting has already been and gone, so there's no one around. A large sign bearing the words CHURCH PARKING, which should have been pointing towards the empty car park across the road, has been turned on its side so that the arrow – very aptly – points towards the sky. Only a few cars pass by on this tree-lined lane, and if it wasn't for the yellow road markings we could be in the Cambrian hills.

We peer through the window at the very old-world interior: centuries-old wooden pews and pulpits, wild-flower floral displays and hymn-tablet wall hangings. The current building dates to around twelve years after Evans's departure to the West to look for the Madogwys, and was built by the very same Samuel Jones.

His slate-roofed house stands just across the graveyard. I take some holiday snaps of John near his old haunt and we pile back into the truck.

THE MAUSOLEUM OF CONTEMPORARY ART

We head downtown to the Mausoleum to set up for tonight's show. John, a natural navigator, seems to know the city like the back of his hand.

Buses pass by, bearing names from places in rural Wales – Gwynedd

Mercy University, Bala Cynwyd, Berwyn and Bryn Mawr – a reminder of Philly's past as a magnet for Welsh Nonconformists. When John came through the city in the early 1790s it was the temporary capital of the US, George Washington was president and the heart of the new republic must have been one of the most exciting places to be for a white European man. The Welsh societies in the city were filled with some of its most influential politicians. Indeed, it's claimed that eighteen of the fifty-six signatories of the Declaration of Independence were of Welsh descent, although only one, Francis Lewis, was born back in the old country.

The Mausoleum is an absurdist arts centre based in a former showroom for tombstones and mausoleums, where Diplo's Mad Decent record label and studio were housed during their most vibrant beginnings. The interior space has a white back wall, so tonight I can project Gwyn A. Williams's film *Madoc: The Making of a Myth* as a support act.

I set up my show and take John out on a sightseeing trip, retracing Sly Stallone's infamous jog as Rocky up the colossal sweep of steps that lead to Philly's official Museum of Art. Rocky was an unlikely character that Stallone had to write for himself as he wasn't getting any acting work from emergent Italian-American directors such as Scorsese and Coppola, who thought he lacked that something or other. Evans was in a similar position to the seventies-era Stallone: unable to secure any backing for his journey, he just created his own solo expedition. John, aping Rocky, looks back in awe at the night-time view of the city's marble and glass skyline from the top of the steps. Various Philadelphia melodies swim around my head, until 'Private Eyes' by Hall and Oates strikes a peculiar note in my mind as I glimpse the reflection of Philadelphia's bright lights in John's own glassy eyes.

'He looks like Count Chocula,' says a large man wearing a baseball cap when I re-enter the Mausoleum half an hour later.

'Who does?' I ask.

He points at John. 'Don't you know Count Chocula?' he offers, feeling the confusion in my vacant expression.

'No,' I reply blankly.

'He was the face of a famous chocolate cereal in the 1980s,' he replies with an air of disbelief. 'Don't you remember the commercial?'

He gets his phone from his jeans and, zapping a request up through the clouds above, sure enough within seconds finds an image of the cartoon count.

'Damn! He *does* look pretty similar. We never had him in Europe,' I venture, by way of excuse. 'Are you going to the show?'

'Yes,' the man replies, scratching his goatee beard. I notice he has a Welsh dragon on his cap. He follows my stare.

'I'm Welsh, so I follow Welsh bands. Well, I'm half Jewish too. I guess I'm American,' he concludes.

I bid farewell to my new wheat-based-snack-eating friend and take John in to warm up for the performance. The new song's coming along nicely:

You zoomed up to Philly,
They'd taught you to make maps,
They showered you with piety,
And pitied any lapse . . .

THREE

RETURN TO PENNEPACK

Having quit his surveying job, the restless John Evans made a grand return from Baltimore to Philadelphia in late February 1793. Once more he stayed at Dr Samuel Jones's family home, but this time no one could hold him back. Pillars of the community came and went, declaring that he was mad: wasn't he aware that the Ohio Indians were at war with the Americans only just beyond Pennsylvania? 'God is my Shield,' replied Evans, as he headed alone into the wilds of the Allegheny Mountains, aiming his nose towards the unexplored West with only one dollar and seventy-five cents to his name.

Avatar John and I plan to follow his fearless trail too, but first there's a small matter of logistics. My driving has been erratic, to say the least, and John is looking more miserable by the day. As the drives from now on will be extremely long, I've made an urgent call to a legend of the wilderness, a frontier man by the name of Joe Puleo, the road manager of the peerless New Jersey band Yo La Tengo who has a sideline in truck-driving unusual loads. His screenplay *Cures for Love* will one day crawl from obscurity and win a multitude of gongs, but in the meantime he is willing to help us out by driving from Indiana with a mysterious truck that we can borrow for the tour. It's rumoured that Bob Marley used it on his last ever American tour, and you can actually sleep in it.

The truck is like the one in Steven Spielberg's first movie, *Duel*, but bigger and blacker. I don't know where Joe found it, but it's a monster. On the back, rather than a large silver tank or an outsized gigantic cargo box with a big logo emblazoned down the side, there's a house. A house shaped like a black box, resembling either a gleaming sideways monolith or a particularly rectangular Winnebago-style motorhome. The interior will accommodate my good self and John on comfortable bunk beds, and there's space enough for guests too. Heck, there's even a kind of rudimentary kitchenette.

As the distances between shows will get longer, Joe has sketched out a rota for night driving which, responsibly, exempts John from duty. Joe plans to come and go as his busy schedule permits. I climb up to the driver's cabin, hoot the horn and follow the trail of Evans into the wilderness.

FOUR

THE LOST CIVILIZATION
OF BEULA

Aka the ghost town of Morgan John Rhys

Overnight, John and I power our way down the highways and skyways, past the blown-out old reactor at Three Mile Island and beyond to the Allegheny Mountains. The sun is making its way in through the blinds of the box we call home, casting a shadow reminiscent of a kitsch 1980s Kim Wilde video. It's time to park up and nap. Eventually I roll out of my bottom-of-the-rung bunk. John is still resting quietly on the top one. I make my way over to the kitchenette and peer through the window, filling the kettle from a gallon bottle of water as I do so.

Outside is a dusty baseball ground with one small rickety stand for spectators. I head out of the door. It's a peaceful summer's day in rural Pennsylvania. All is quiet. WELCOME TO EBENSBURG, declares a sign at the side of the road.

So, we are on the outskirts of town.

I go back inside, get the coffee brewing and wake up John.

Ebensburg is the capital of Cambria County, PA. It's a county that one Morgan John Rhys helped to carve out from the burgeoning state of Pennsylvania by persuading a host of Welsh people to leave Wales and settle in the promised land of democracy and equality: the United States of America, and more specifically in the promised land of Beula. This was a utopian town, based on the values of freedom, the New Testament and learning. It had a well-stocked library at its heart, highly unusual for a small pioneer town.

Rhys (who would soon change his name to Rhees and occasionally to Reese), an enterprising evangelist and witness to the French Revolution in Paris, was too radical a Jacobin for late-eighteenth-century Wales. He left after his periodical, *Y Cylchgrawn Cynmraeg* [*sic*] – 'The Welsh Magazine' – was shut down by the authorities after five issues. It was a political hot potato and no printing house could produce it without severe repercussions. Since the violent uprising in revolutionary France, the authorities were cracking down on dissenters. John Evans had fled the British Isles before Rhys with perfect timing. Rhys had written of Madog and of Evans's proposed journey in the first issue of *Y Cylchgrawn Cynmraeg*, and in time he was to have a decisive influence on Evans's travels.

Morgan John Rhys was a man of strong political values, far from the pious teetotaller of the nineteenth-century Methodist archetype. He was more of a pragmatic beer-drinking Baptist. By observing his thoughts, along with those of other contemporaries such as Iolo Morganwg, we can begin to get a feel for the mindset of John Evans himself, another of his peer group.

Rhys arrived in America in October 1794, two years after Evans, and, having spent a few weeks exploring the northern states of Vermont and New York, immediately set off on an anti-slavery preaching tour of the Southern states – all the while on the lookout for a tract of land where he could set up an ideal town, where the poor and persecuted theological minds of Wales could settle and prosper, free from the shackles of landowners, the Church of England and the English monarchy.

Having travelled far and wide through the Carolinas, Georgia, Tennessee, Kentucky and Ohio, Rhys finally reached his promised land around a hundred miles east of today's Pittsburgh, in a place tucked up high in the Allegheny Mountains. In all probability it reminded him of the tree-lined hills of Wales, but it was a disastrous choice when you consider all the lands he passed over. Under the trees lay the rockiest of grounds, useless for crops and pasture, and the Welsh settlers, numbering almost 500, were unable to make a living even within the minimum 64-acre plots.

Faced with a bleak future, a typically Welsh denominational struggle took place. One Lloyd Rhys formed firstly a breakaway independent chapel, spurning Morgan John Rhys's utopian non-denominational meeting place, and eventually built the new town of Ebensburg in 1804, inaugurated in memory of his son Ebenezer. Ebensburg narrowly won an election to become county capital, signalling the death knell for the settlement of Beula, which soon perished and is now a ghost town in the forest.

I slurp some Iolo coffee in the truck, crack some jokes with ol' John and drive into town, where I hover, engine grumbling like a giant contented black bear, outside an Italian restaurant, which seems like the liveliest place around. The friendly restaurateur, who's watering his plants on the pavement, calls out some directions and we head out of town in search of the Old Beula Road.

BEULA

Thou shalt no more be termed Forsaken; neither shall thy land any more be termed Desolate: but thou shalt be called Hephzibah, and thy land Beulah (Isaiah 62:4)

State Route 3034, affectionately known as Old Beula Road, is a winding unmarked road that weaves through forest and makes a nice change from the uniform grid of the town plan and most of the geometric interstate roads. I drive slowly, John navigates and we keep a lookout for a ghost town through the windows and a home-made mirror system involving a periscope and the Kim Wilde metal blinds in the back.

Eventually we pass a low standing stone by the side of the road, adorned with a metal plaque that's shaped like a Heinz baked beans label. We stop the truck and jump out to investigate. It reads:

A TOWN LAID OUT BY REVEREND
MORGAN JOHN RHYS (REESE) IN 1797 AFTER
THE PLAN OF PHILADELPHIA. ABOUT
THREE HUNDRED INHABITANTS,
PRINCIPALLY WELSH, SETTLED HERE. THE TOWN
HAD TWO HOTELS, A STORE, MILL, SCHOOL,
CHURCH AND CIRCULATING LIBRARY OF SIX
HUNDRED VOLUMES. HERE WAS LOCATED THE
FIRST POST OFFICE FOR CAMBRIA COUNTY
AND BEULA WAS DESIGNATED THE FIRST
POLLING PLACE FOR HOLDING ELECTIONS
FOR THIS REGION BEFORE CAMBRIA
COUNTY EXISTED. THE CEMETERY IS
LOCATED NORTH OF THIS POINT.

ERECTED BY THE CAMBRIA COUNTY
HISTORICAL SOCIETY
1936

71

Some printed text on a piece of paper has been attached with tape just above the plaque to deter meth-heads. It reads:

This Plaque is made of Steel and has no real value

We climb over a gate and start making our way up the unpaved road to the cemetery. A few cars pass by. NO TRESPASSING signs start to appear on the trees either side of the road.

Suddenly a car skids to a stop by the gate and a woman gets out with some urgency, shouting, 'Hello, this is a private road!'

Once I have explained our mission and introduced her to John, she relaxes.

'Oh, these signs are just to stop the kids going up to the cemetery and getting high and breaking stuff,' she says, then adds, 'I'm a Hughes. My family lived in Beula and we still own this section of the land. I was just checking up. The cemetery's the only thing left of the old settlement. Someone spotted some people here and phoned me up. Have fun, guys!'

So, having met one of the descendants of the original inhabitants, we proceed up the hill a few hundred yards to a clearing in the trees. The sunlight paints stripes of light on to the old gravestones. Many are graves of infants, and it seems heartbreaking that these second-generation children didn't go on to have a better life after all. Still, the crickets chirp and the birds sing and we find the grave of another John Evans, so we pose for photographs, then return down the hill to the truck, leaving behind us the last traces of Morgan John Rhys's personal utopia amidst the swaying trees of the mountains.

NANTY GLO

Back in the truck we snake down the valley and in a handful of miles emerge in Nanty Glo ('Coal Valley'), which like its Welsh namesake is a post-industrial village in a steep valley with a tradition of trade union activism. Its public library has pride of place on the high street, and it is an unexpected treat for us weary travellers suddenly to feel as if we have been transported to some kind of approximation of home.

We head first to the Liberty Café to see what's going on in town, only to discover that the population has halved since the last mine closed in the 1980s. It's towns like these that have been supplying foot soldiers for the 'War on Terror', and we run into some veterans of the Gulf and Iraq wars, who happen to be of Welsh descent, at the café.

Warm welcomes and generosity seem to be consistent hallmarks of Americans' response to visitors. It proves no different here. They share an urn of coffee with us, as a kind man of German descent, sporting an Abraham Lincoln beard, offers us a plate of muffins and questions us about our trip. Photos of the town during its industrial heyday decorate the walls. The veterans paint a bleak picture of its decline. But it's heartening that the community has come together voluntarily to open this café and to keep the main street alive.

Evans, I explain, was heading through the Allegheny range en route to Fort Pitt. It took him a fortnight to cross the mountains from Philadelphia to present-day Pittsburgh, but there we shall follow him – though at a much faster speed. Travelling in the US was slow work in the 1790s, even between the major cities. Overland freight would be drawn by oxen as often as by horse. The era of the tolled turnpike was yet to begin in Pennsylvania, and even when it dawned, horse-drawn carriages would often sink to their hubs in impassable mud that in summer would turn into an unbearable cloud of dust and mosquitoes. Walking would have been the most practical mode of transport for a fit young man. The canals, railroads and steamboats that would revolutionize the occupation and trade routes of America were still a figment of the future imagination.

We finish our coffee, buy a Nanty Glo 'Coal County' baseball cap for John and hop back into the truck, tooting and waving our good-byes as we drive into the pleasant green valley, past the roadside fruit stalls that lie just beyond the toxic rim of the town.

FIVE

THE INTERVENTIONIST DENTIST
AND
THE PITTSBURGH PROMENADE

Do you believe in an interventionist dentist?

One has just peered into my mouth with a torch.

'Oh my God, I'm gonna use this guy as an example of why socialized medicine doesn't work. It's a disaster in here!' he says.

There's an ideological battle going on in my mouth. I fully intend to defend universal healthcare, but a cotton-wool swab is jammed between my gums and the inside of my left cheek. Enraged, I try to leave. John, by hard stare and willpower, pushes me back into my seat.

A thought bubble appears above my head but is obscured by the dentist's lamp, so he doesn't catch it. It reads:

Dentistry in Wales and the European Union in general is not socialized enough. Administered as a patchwork of independent practices, some accept subsidized patients on low incomes and focus rightly on clinical dentistry over the largely aesthetic concerns of the cosmetic dentist, but others opt out fully into the private sector – it's a mess. Unlike, say, the Cuban system, where the police will arrest you and escort you to the nationalized dentist if you're caught out with bad-looking teeth, there's a lack of uniformity. People are largely accepting, however, of the ragged natural beauty of an uneven mouthful of teeth, and some of our best-known popular faces sport craggy smiles, bursting with personality. Which is key to imagining John Evans and the people he met in the Americas of the late eighteenth century, before the rise of cosmetic dentistry changed the face of the subcontinent.

Dr Zanne Wedelstaedt talks, drills, X-rays, signs insurance claims, scratches his head, ties his laces and picks up his coffee cup like a living movie montage, all the while barking commands at his formidable yet hesitant assistants. He seems like an amalgam of Al Pacino and Joe Pesci. Short, stocky and quick on his feet; it feels to me as though he must be dealing with several patients at once, our seats divided by thin grey plastic partitions that fail to dampen any sigh or sound. Negotiating around the screens, he strides from seat to seat so swiftly that his young charges can barely keep up. Cleaning a tooth here, filling a hole there, leaving detailed delegated instructions behind him.

I booked him via the Korean palmtop. He had by far the most distinct and heroic logo, which reminded me of a Communist hammer and sickle motif (but depicting crossed dental tools) and gave the impression that he might be a fellow supporter of free social services for all. The design was headed with the reassuring motto: Zanne Can!

I was all for putting up with the pain for the next few weeks, but I wasn't a fun guy to be around any more and John insisted. He is sitting on one of the few unoccupied dental chairs. He never complains, and I'm fairly embarrassed that I'm giving in to a relatively minor complaint, compared to what the old-timers had to endure. I once read of a nineteenth-century Welsh pioneer in Patagonia who, when faced with almost certain death, had to slice himself open and remove his own cursed appendix – then stitch himself back together again. Evans, however, as far as we know, was still in fine health at this Pittsburghian point in his previous life.

Wedelstaedt studies the X-ray.

'Well, see this little tail here? I'm gonna have to go right into the root canal and take it out. So I'll suck out your existing crown with this piece of apparatus, drill into your gums, then pluck out the root.'

More thought bubbles, ignored. I nod.

The industrial-looking vacuum machine manages to suck out the infected crown, making a large BANG! At least it's painless, my gums successfully numbed by anaesthetic.

'So you're a singer, right?'

I nod again.

'What kind of music do you play?'

'Kimb of melobig bob zongs,' I dribble.

'Oh right, nice.' He drills deep into my gums.

'That's enough for today,' he says afterwards. 'I'll see you again in the morning, 8 a.m. I'm putting this kinda putty in the hole. Leave it three hours or so, then you can eat. No cheese, though, or pizza, or anything sticky that could take out the putty, all right?'

I venture out into the warm evening, with a Vicodin prescription in hand and John on my shoulders. Waiting for a taxi to come and pick me up, too drowsy to drive, I browse in a second-hand music shop in a boiling-hot asphalt strip mall.

'Can I help you?'

I realize that I can barely speak, so I nod and smile salivally.

I play some Van Halen on a synthesized keyboard, then notice the cab pulling in.

*

It's a night off the stage and out of the truck tonight. We get to stay in a fancy hotel. It has free laundry, cable TV, breakfast, an outdoor pool, unlimited apples and coffee, plus a complimentary copy of *USA Today*. Whoa!

I stockpile some apples and sleep off the anaesthetic for a few hours.

Later on I cross the seven-acre parking lot with John towards a gaggle of themed restaurants with glowing, all-colour Comic Sans signs.

At pains to avoid pizza, we choose the Japanese Grill from a selection of Thai (closed; it's almost ten), Tex-Mex (unappealing graphics) and Unspecified (banal-looking mounds of landscaped meat in the photograph – not suitable for vegetarians).

We sit on a horseshoe-shaped bench with the seven other customers (two couples and one birthday trio) whilst a smiling chef in a commanding central position sets the food, and himself, alight. Repeatedly, he claps two meat cleavers together loudly, then douses his elongated chef's hat in fluid and goes up in flames. It's a great gag, like watching a Man or Astro-man? show, but later, when a waiter brings him the wrong amount of rice, he seems angry. In fact, he seems pretty uptight overall. He's been on fire too many times tonight already. John looks nonplussed.

The real John Evans would have been walking for the most part through largely pristine forest in those days, dependent on the

generosity of the families he crossed paths with, as the influence of European settlers diminished with every step he took west. He may well have passed this very spot, craving the shelter and warmth that Pittsburgh promised, after his two-week hike.

FANGS A LOT

It's 7.30 a.m. My taxi is late, and there doesn't seem to be any public transport in this out-of-town island of commerce in the black-tar sea. I toy with stealing an unaccompanied Segway when a besuited limo driver, who's in the vicinity for some other reason, agrees to take me.

'You realize I'm only doing this because I believe people should be able to go from A to B to Z? You could never even afford me usually, and I'm not even going to charge you. It's your lucky day.'

'Thanks so much,' I say. I tip heavily.

Dr Zanne drills deeper into my gums. Two assistants are leaning over me too. I can feel the intensity of the machinery in my bones, when . . .

'Oh!'

The early-morning shot of anaesthesia finally kicks in . . . Stars/ time/bubbles/love . . .

Having been revived, the hole in my mouth apparently filled and crowned and a brand-new one ripped open in my pocket, I find myself safely back at the music shop across the street, playing the synthesizer again and free from pain. It's show day in Pittsburgh.

We drive the truck to Mount Washington to view the source of the Ohio River. Up on the bluff a beautiful panorama opens up below us: an incredible view of the whole city, rising out of the triangular convergence of the Monongahela and Allegheny rivers, which together create a third, great river – the Ohio – that flows towards us and runs all the way to the Mississippi: the same great river that served John Evans's journey so well as he harnessed its mighty current into the American interior.

On the way we get directions from three factory workers in overalls taking a break in the hot sunshine. They look like they've come straight out of a Robert Frank photo. One of the men says it's considered the third-best skyline view in America.

'Where are you guys from?' asks another, then tells me that his great-great-great-grandfather was one of the eighteen signatories of Welsh heritage who signed the Declaration of American Independence. What are the chances, eh?

SIX

FORT PITT

I take John for lunch at the Monterey Bay Fish Grotto atop Mount Washington to celebrate my pain-free mouth. The Grotto's ballroom-like interior is filled floor to ceiling with hand-painted lush tropical greenery, parrots, fauna and flora. We can only afford the coffee, and in any case the left half of my face is still drooping from the combined effects of Novocain and Vicodin. I ask for a straw.

We sit by the window, right on top of the cliff and another fourteen floors up. It has one of the best, and surely the highest, views of the cityscape. We look down at a cluster of skyscrapers that serve as a magnificent backdrop to the site of the fort that Evans would have visited, which is in clear view from our window. Vertigo spins us into the vortex of the coffee and we emerge at Fort Pitt, March 1793.

PITTSBURGH WITHOUT PYNCHON

When John Evans arrived here, the town was less than a decade old and only just emerging from being a village. Pots and pans would be clanging and horses braying along to the music of construction. Farmyard animals would be jostling for position with humans. The smell of the pigsty would battle for supremacy with gunpowder, burning wood and the mud of the riverbeds that surrounded this narrow peninsular settlement. Thirty years previously the original Fort Pitt had been on the frontline of the Seven Years War between the British and everyone else.

The political tremors of the recent past would evidently have been reverberating for Evans, and the violent current that ran through the frontier continued as the US now took to fighting the local tribes, and by proxy the British to the north. In an era of massacres Fort Pitt was not an easy-going vacation location. And it was only a few months since George Washington had expressed dissatisfaction at the continuing success of the tribes of the Ohio in stalling US expansion, signifying a more determined military effort. Evans stayed here for a month, with a Mr C. Wheeler, in order to wait for the spring waters to rise up enough for an easy passage down the Ohio River by boat as far as Limestone, Kentucky.

Still, Fort Pitt was a magnet to a steady flow of fearless young adventurers as it was a gateway not only to British Canada to the north but to war-torn Ohio to the west, where the Shawnee were still strong. Kentucky lay to the south, and way beyond to the far west lay the mysterious vast territory of Spanish Louisiana. It would have been an exciting time for Evans. He had left the pious and controlling Welsh Phillygentsia and the East Coast Baptists behind him. They had done everything they could to dissuade him from taking this journey, but he was in control now, a lone agent with limitless possibilities ahead. Indeed, not a trace of any missionary ambition appears again in his correspondence.

This was the last chance for Evans to act on his previous intention of reaching the Madogwys by way of the Great Lakes and the Canadian North. But when the river rose he boarded the boat to Kentucky, choosing instead the far riskier route through the American interior, one that crossed many war zones, tribal-controlled lands and the Mosquito Belt.

In an attempt to recreate that momentous occasion, I take John down to the Allegheny River. He spots a courting couple taking their speedboat out of the water, and I ask if we can borrow it. Unbelievably, they agree: adults, kids, dogs – they all just seem to cave in to John's deadpan charisma wherever we go. I place the recreated old explorer down on a passenger seat and take the controls for a few turns of the river. I have no idea what I'm doing, and the courting couple – who are called Jan and Dean, just like the 1960s surf duo – don't seem to have much idea either. They stare at me blankly when I ask them how it works. I'd say they are in their mid thirties, and they tell me that later they're going to steer the boat to moorings outside the Pittsburgh Pirates baseball stadium to sit down for a fine meal before taking in a game. The river breeze catches in John's coarse felt hair and I detect a longing for tomorrow and the long drive west to Destiny.

Only one thing stands between us and that road: a packed show at the Club Café tonight. They say folks have driven here from as far as Cleveland, Ohio. *Mercy!*

So you went down to Pittsburgh
And waited for the waters to rise
And set sail down the Ohio,
With a lost tribe on your mind.

When you said that you loved me,
I knew it wasn't true,
I've two hundred unread messages,
But not a single note from you.

SEVEN

THE MAGICAL MAYOR
OF
RIO GRANDE;
OR
MOST LIKELY: GOLF AND FREEMASONRY IN LIBERAL AMERICA

And/Or: Even Deadheads get into office

The mayor arranges a police escort for our mega-truck, which meets us outside the city limits. I say city, but I suppose it's more of a tiny rural college town: it has a population of 810 when the students are away.

It's a hallucinatory experience driving into town, with Welsh flags hanging from every lamp post. We are taken to a central parking lot, where the Deadhead Democratic mayor Robert Easter greets us with huge polystyrene cups of coffee. Rio (pronounced Rye-O) is an island of blue liberal thinking in the red sea of rural Ohio Republicanism. It's positioned twenty miles north-west of the French-influenced Ohio River town of Gallipolis. John Evans in all probability did not make it this far from the river, unless he left his boat for an impromptu hunting expedition; in which case he would not have seen another European soul here in 1793.

We sleep off the coffee on the truck's benches and at eleven I walk around the block to the Madog Center for Welsh Studies, giving John a piggyback. We are welcomed by the director, Jeanne Jones Jindra, and a Welsh teacher, Lisa Jones, who fled to the States a year ago when her father became a YouTube phenomenon: a video of him cursing a referee during a televised rugby game had gone viral (so viral that he got an album deal).

We ask them about Madog (they are agnostic), and in turn we are interviewed by some local newspapers. Then the police show up again. Inexplicably, the cops arrest John just to freak me out. The prankster mayor, who's in tears of laughter, isn't of Welsh descent, but he reckons a great number of the population are. He also pays the cops' wages, so they follow his every command.

The town's most famous Welshman was Bob Evans, founder of the famed eponymous country-restaurant franchise. When John is eventually returned by the laughing policemen, we are taken for lunch to the original restaurant just a mile out of town. Here, under a perfect powder-blue sky, is an idyllic vision of the white-picket-fence Midwest, evoking Grant Wood's *American Gothic* painting, or even *Babe*, the movie. There are rolling hills, the fields are a manicured green, and well-brushed horses graze with a sense of luxurious purpose. The Bob Evans wooden barn that bears his signature in red is a picturesque slice of white-bread Americana. We order the vegetarian option whilst John sits at the dining bar and enjoys the attention of the waiters.

Ohio's most awkward son, Scott Walker, sang the most beautiful song, 'The Lights of Cincinnati', for his old home town. Scott fled to existential Europe, but we're about to make the six-hour trip to the city for our next show.* We jump back into the mayor's pickup, with John perched on the roof, and drive back towards the truck over the speed bumps of Rio for a quick coffee stop at his house before leaving.

The mayor takes me down to his basement garage to get his gas guns: large bazooka-like drainage pipes that he fills with aerosol gas and that, when he sets the fumes alight – BAM! – shoot a deafening sonic boom through this wooded rural idyll. One of his roles as mayor and champion of his community is to shoot a pipe after every goal scored by the local soccer team, so that everyone knows about it.

It's election year, and he despairs at the polarization of American politics. His garage is filled with the iconographic posters of collegiate America: Che Guevara, Obama and the Grateful Dead's skull motif take pride of place. Charismatic, friendly and generous he might be, but how on earth did this idealistic, tattooed and pierced man become mayor?

'I play golf and come from a family of Freemasons,' he deadpans.

Freemasonry was something that both John Evans and Iolo Morganwg flirted with, but that was the 1790s and it was all the rage in the Old and New Worlds to make up weird rites and practise them with friends, and besides, they didn't have cinema, pop music or the Internet. It was a rite of passage, like being in a jam band.

But what is it to today's America? Isn't it a weird, right-wing, exclusive cult that facilitates corruption and undermines democratic society?

* Those interested in the more logistical aspects of the touring life may note that, just like in the song, we did see the lights of Cincinnati through pine trees: we made a stop at a parkland RV sewage facility to empty the truck's septic tank before entering the city, and from the mountainside we glimpsed the majestic orange glow of the hilly, Rome-like metropolis.

EIGHT

CINCINNATI

With Jay All Day, Skyline Chili and Boom Bip

The truck chugs in late to Cincinnati, we park up on Main Street in the Over-the-Rhine district, find a bar that sells whiskey sours, and tear into the night. We awake early and grizzly, stumble out of the truck and roll ten yards up the street into the Iris Book Café.

'Hi, I'm Jay All Day,' says Jay All Day, MC, local radio host and force of nature. 'What can I get you two gentlemen?'

In a minute we are friends.

The coffee wakes us up and before you know it we are being interviewed by Jay right there at the café bar for her radio show, or website, or whatever other magical medium of her own making that is one stage beyond all currently known media. She's such a screaming comet of energy that I'm starting to think I'm falling into the coffee vortex again.

Our waltzing host then leads us through her incredible bookshop, where we're bombarded by stimuli – text, image, music, vapour – until we reach the courtyard, where I have a passive cigarette. Before I can let out a howl from the hill, I'm standing in the best second-hand-record shop on Earth and meeting Mark Markiewicz, the bearded (I mean beard of the decade: you could live in it) proprietor of Another Part of the Forest, named for Shakespeare's *As You Like*

It. Its walls are emblazoned with murals depicting key scenes from the Bard's pastoral comedy, and the comedy continues in the headings of the vinyl bins – 'Secular Choral', 'Cheesecake', 'Germanic Wood-wind', 'Korean Jazz' – which house over 20,000 records, comics and – for the cinephile – DVDs and videos from all known lands.

I pick up a three-dollar album of Native American songs, recorded by Californian students in the 1960s; two little-known late-period albums by the legendary moustachioed Italian disco producer Giorgio Moroder; a fifteen-album spoken-word *Life* magazine box set of the history of the USA from the seventeenth century onwards; and an album called *Fillet of Soul*, the distinctive cover of which depicts a soul diva mermaid with a large Afro and the body of a fish.

John, who's been casually reclining in the German pop section, reminds me, by the power of telepathy, that I have a show to set up. We leave the magical realm of the record shop, cross the courtyard into the Iris Book Café, invite Jay All Day to our concert and pick up the second-hand books we bought earlier in our first rush of excitement, including the sensational-at-99-cents *Maps: A Historical Survey of Their Study and Collecting*, by R. A. Skelton.

We head out to the streets of Cincinnati, refreshed and inspired, having been showered in attention and personality, fine music and ideas, our pineal (third eye) glands thoroughly scrubbed in speedy caffeine.

For John Evans, Cincinnati would also have been a chance to recover his senses for a few days in what was then a tiny brand-new settlement of around 200 people, dominated by an equally new wooden structure: the US military base of Fort Washington. Having travelled almost 300 miles down the Ohio by boat, he landed first in Limestone, Kentucky, now known as Maysville.

Kentucky was a new state, freshly carved out of Virginia only the previous year, and it marked the western reaches of the USA in this period. We can speculate that it was safer for Evans to cut inland through Bourbon County and the wilderness towards Cincinnati. The North-west Indian War was still raging, and the Ohio lands north of the river were under tribal control, armed to the hilt by the British from the north, so this is a possible explanation for his overland detour south of the Ohio River. He may have been curious to investigate the new European settlements in Kentucky, but offers no further details in his meagre correspondence.

According to the diary of David Jones, a Philadelphia-based Baptist minister of Welsh descent who had been a frontiersman (and was one of the people who tried to talk Evans out of heading alone into this chaotic war-torn continent), Evans had been furnished in Philadelphia with a letter of commendation by President George Washington himself. There is no corroborating evidence of the existence of this letter, and it may be another of Evans's exaggerations, but whatever the case may have been, the gates of the city opened for him, as they always seemed to during his stay on US territory. Just as in Fort Pitt, he was warmly received for a few days' rest – this time by an Irishman, Brigadier General Wilkinson, who would play a continuing pivotal role in Evans's future. Time has revealed that Wilkinson was effectively a Spanish double agent,* well placed to suggest that Evans should proceed on his journey towards the Spanish-controlled territories that lay to the west.

Within a few years, when it had been granted its charter as a village, Cincinnati became a magnet for the Welsh, as new immigrants and

---

* Actually triple: he was also scheming for an independent Kentucky, of which he would be president.

refugees from the troubled Beula settlement upriver descended in droves on the Paddy's Run district near the Miami River. But Evans was never to return.

Tonight's show is in the Contemporary Arts Center in Cincinnati, a building that, famously, is architect Zaha Hadid's first completed large-scale commission. It features a staircase constructed entirely without right angles, built by a roller-coaster company, and a brushed-concrete floor which merges seamlessly with the pavement outside and eventually curves upwards to act as the spine of the whole building.

This building has an extra resonance for me: in the 1990s Hadid won an architectural competition to design a landmark opera house* to accommodate the Welsh National Opera company in Cardiff, my home city. It would have been her first major commission, instantly making it a building of major international significance.

'We actually have a lot of visitors who come from out of town, just to visit the building,' the CAC's curator, Molly O'Toole, tells me. 'And it's really done a lot to show the progressive current in the city.'

There's a 'History of the Music Video' exhibition on at the moment, which gives us the opportunity to place John in front of a camera and insert him into the famed animated video for 'Take on Me', the inaugural and biggest hit of Norwegian pop trio A-ha. After cracking up with laughter, we head down to the space where John and I will play the show, which is to be one of the best attended of the tour.

---

* The intended design was ultimately shelved, after an outcry which Hadid believes was sexist and xenophobic. A modified design was eventually built in Guangzhou, China. You snooze, you lose.

I get to sing the latest verse of '100 Unread Messages':

You left olde Kentucky
And sailed to the west,
Stopped in Cincinnati,
Dined with all the best . . .

The Cleveland crew have travelled far to be with us again, and my friend Boom Bip, who was once based here, has come back from California to DJ after the show. It's a great night. Even Jay All Day shows up, and it soon transpires that she's equally Jay at night too.

'John Evans!' she shouts out at full volume from the crowd. John remains tranquil.

'I love that "American Interior" song you did,' a baseball-capped Ohioan comments after the show, referring to one of my more serious numbers, as he walks out of the venue.

'Wow, thanks,' I reply earnestly, as everyone seems to thank profusely in this city.

'Yes, it's hilarious,' he continues. 'I laughed so hard when I heard that one.'

Uncertain of how I should react to this cultural misinterpretation (the line between the earnest power ballad and the parody song is by its very nature pretty fuzzy), I am unable to resist joining in the merriment. 'Thank you so much,' I say.

Maybe it's my accent that sets him off again: 'You're welcome so much!' he laughs back as I gather up John, who's fast asleep already – laid out flat on the stage under a coat. The further from the coast I go, the more exotic I seem to become. And the more elaborate the American art of politeness grows to be.

We head out to the truck, ready for our trip into old Spanish territory. It's been a joyous day roller-coasting the hills and modernist stairwells of Cincinnati. 'Thank you so very much,' I sing to the wind.

'You're welcome!' cries the entire population of the metropolitan area as we cross back over the bridge into Kentucky.

NINE

THE BRANDENBURG STONE
OF
KENTUCKY

As we proceed westwards along the grey concrete snake through the humid Southern night, we cross the great Ohio into Newport, Kentucky, and drive past the 200-year-old Southgate House, the birthplace of the tommy gun. It was here that Super Furry Animals once played in the ballroom to an origami-throwing audience whilst my drummer friend Pat drank herself into a soft coma at the bar with members of the Soledad Brothers.

Onwards we roll, roaring down the 71 towards the state of Kentucky's biggest city, Louisville. John Evans would have had to spend time here, in the late spring of 1793, as the river plunges into the falls of the Ohio and his boat would have been carried overland – *Fitzcarraldo* style – through what was then an emerging settlement.

Throughout America in this period, ear-witness accounts were circulating about Native American tribes speaking Welsh, and in the Southern states, forts deemed to be of Welsh origin were being discovered. In Wales, with reports of Welsh habitation steadily trickling through from the Americas, Madog was becoming a tangible hero.

Fleeing Wales from religious persecution in the seventeenth

century, the minister and general lunatic Morgan Jones claimed he was saved from the throes of certain death just by speaking the language. Having been captured and condemned to death in southern Virginia by hostile Tuscaroras, he reported that, during this 1669 event, upon saying a few last words in Welsh he was overheard and understood by a visiting member of the Doeg tribe, who took him back to their forest for protection, where he then lived with them for four months, preaching the New Testament in Welsh.

This account was not printed until 1740, when the British and Spanish were at war again and any validation of a British land claim in America was useful propaganda. Gradually, throughout the eighteenth century, these rumours and claims multiplied as Europeans reported sightings of Welsh-speaking tribes. Of course, much as the Greeks called non-Greeks *barbaroi*, or barbarians, as all they seemed to say was 'Baa baa baa', most of these witnesses didn't speak Welsh, so any American language with unusual consonants would have sounded Welsh (which is itself just an old Saxon word for 'foreign'). These double-Dutch stories were now augmented by reports from a French explorer, Pierre Gaultier de Varennes, sieur de La Vérendrye, of a tribe in the Upper Missouri basin who possessed a lighter skin tone than usual.

A series of stone forts in various stages of disrepair were found throughout the Southern states, including one at Fort Mountain near Chattanooga (upon climbing this, during a tour of the American South with ace surf act Y Niwl, I once disturbed a rattlesnake, but that's another story). This particular fort was claimed to resemble Dolwyddelan Castle in North Wales and convinced American Madog theorists that it was confirmation of the Madogwys tribe's gradual movement from the Gulf of Mexico towards their eventual Mandan existence near Canada. Today we can perceive this as a racist assumption, in that European, slave-owning settlers could not fathom how indigenous tribes were capable of erecting these complex stone forts. Carbon-dating technology has since corroborated that these sites were built centuries before Madog's supposed era.

Yet another war between the two colonial titans Britain and Spain prompted the publication in 1791, to much excitement, of a further book on Madog by Dr John Williams. The myth of Madog now became what Gwyn A. Williams would call, in his Madog book, 'an idea that walks', boosting the confidence of a new cabal of Welsh separatists already high on the doctrines of religious and class freedom seeping from America and the imminent new republic in France. The emergence of Madog handed them an instant Welsh empire in the Americas and confirmed this tiny Celtic nation as a potential world power.

The final 'proof' was a visit to London in 1791 by William Bowles, an Irish American who had married a Cherokee wife and called himself a chief. He relayed second-hand anecdotes to the salivating Welsh faction of the Bull's Head pub (which by this time included both Iolo Morganwg and John Evans) and recounted the stories told to him by friends of friends who had seen the white-skinned 'Padoucas' and their Welsh-style boats and houses in the northern Missouri.

Iolo put 2 + 7 together to make a rickety 10, and confirmed that 'Padoucas' (actually a word of French origin) was derived from the name of the Welsh tribe Madogwys. John Evans's young mind would have been whipped into a frenzy of possibilities by these tales, and *Y Madogwys au Angau* ('The Madogwys or Death') became his motto, based on *Fraternité, ou la Mort!* ('Brotherhood or Death'), the rallying cry of the French revolutionaries.

The year 1791 saw another of Iolo's more interesting inventions. He developed a twenty-character alphabet for written Welsh which he called Coelbren y Beirdd ('The Belief Tablet of the Bards'), loosely based on an amalgam of the ogam script that the old Celts used to carve on standing stones and his own vivid imagination. This would have been fine in itself, and an interesting addition to the emerging character alphabets of the modern world, but of course Iolo insisted that this was an ancient Druidic script that he had rediscovered, and backed it up with an ingenious yet bizarre-looking wooden contraption containing rows of spools on which he claimed the Druids would have created their texts, rotating the spools to create complex verses, or *cywyddau*, on demand – like a primitive form of app.

Once a myth is unleashed, much like a libellous front-page newspaper article, the truth or the apology is never broadcast quite as prominently. In that sense, Madogian theories and the demented forgeries of Iolo Morganwg are still influential today, and even prompted the History Channel (which is part-owned by Disney) in the second decade of the twenty-first century to link the Brandenburg Stone, an inscribed limestone slab in Kentucky, to Madog himself.

In 1912, just a few miles downriver from the falls of the Ohio in Louisville, north-west of modern-day Fort Knox, farmer Craig Crecelius was ploughing his field when he unearthed an unusual stone tablet that seemed to contain some kind of script carved into the rock. He took the stone home and spent the next half-century trying to decipher the history of this artefact, inviting the curious and the academic to visit his home to take a look. In the 1960s the stone was placed in the Meade County Public Library in Brandenburg, where its script was identified by Jon Whitfield as Coelbren, which he innocently thought was an ancient Welsh script. (Nice one, Iolo.)

This linked the stone to a further chain of carvings discovered in the Southern states. Was this the final proof of Madog's unstoppable passage through America?

In the 1990s, photographs of the stone were sent to the mysterious Arthurian Research Foundation in Wales, where the script was translated as:

Towards strength (to promote unity), divide the land we are spread over, purely (or justly) between offspring in wisdom.

In time, the fact that this script was not invented until 1791 became apparent. Furthermore, if Madog *had* existed and had landed in the Americas in 1170, he would have been writing more or less in modern Welsh, using the Latin script. In 1999 the stone was moved to the 'Myths and Legends' exhibit at the Interpretive Center in the Falls of Ohio State Park.

With the mythical link to Madog in tatters, it suddenly became viable that this stone was from the *real* historical hand of John Evans. Here was a close friend and colleague of Iolo Morganwg, who had come to America only a year after Iolo's 'discovery' of the Coelbren alphabet, so it's fair to assume that Evans would have been aware of and capable of mastering this simple script. He most certainly passed close to the site of the Crecelius discovery (now a limestone quarry), and had he stopped over for the night here, forty miles downriver from the Ohio Falls, what was a young man to do whilst resting up on a bluff? Before the age of texting, surely it would have been fun to carve some Druidic graffiti into the soft rock.

There are some serious flaws in this hypothesis, however. Firstly, the script carved into the stone has only a very superficial resemblance to Iolo's Coelbren alphabet, which I taught myself in my early twenties; and secondly, it does not spell anything out in the Welsh language, my mother tongue.

Given that these stone carvings are prevalent throughout Southern and Midwestern US, with over fifty-five in known existence, it's now clear that they must be part of a vast, ancient Native American civilization. Is this not reason enough to celebrate the Brandenburg stone? Or is it deemed to require some kind of European validation to become a historically relevant object? Regardless, this fascinating stone is currently back on display at the Meade County Public Library.

Madog seems to be slipping away from our grasp, but John Evans is becoming more substantial by the day. As we leave the mega-cities of the East Coast and start to encounter the small towns and villages of the interior, we find further traces of him. The town plans have changed less, the archives can be contained in a few boxes, and I feel that we are about to start meeting people who will help us in our quest to unravel the John Evans story.

TEN

THE GENESIS
OF
DON JUAN EVANS

And the New Madrid Media Quake of 1990

When John Evans landed in New Madrid in the summer of 1793, he was literally entering another realm. Evans had sailed out of the Ohio and into the giant waterway of the Mississippi, which drains the North American continent into the Gulf of Mexico and the Caribbean beyond. Here, emerging into what would become Huckleberry Finn territory, near Cairo, and sailing south to New Madrid, he was to face one of the biggest crises of his journey, but first there was the small matter of changing his identity.

When Evans set foot on the western bank of the Mississippi, he had crossed from the USA into Spanish-controlled Louisiana, a vast country sometimes known as New Spain, engulfing a third of today's Land of the Free. There, under the jurisdiction of the king of Spain, he undertook his latest transformation by taking an oath to his new king and changing his name officially to Don Juan Evans.

With its prestigious name, New Madrid was destined for greatness by the colonial Spanish of Louisiana. It was at the centre point of a multitude of continental trade routes and would no doubt have continued its development at the pace of New Orleans and St Louis, but for a force far stronger than that of the Spanish or American empires which intervened in the most dramatic fashion, condemning this town to a different destiny: that of a sleepy, friendly village of a few hundred people, where cotton is still picked and turned into bales at the local cotton gin and where the descendants of the French river-men of yore still hunt bullfrogs for their legs. It is nestled in a bend of the great Mississippi, forty-two miles south of the Ohio confluence, and squashed between two of the unfriendliest tectonic plates known to coexist in the continental US.

The New Madrid fault system runs for over 120 miles along a stretch of the Mississippi that cuts through the states of Arkansas and Missouri on its west bank and Tennessee, Kentucky and Illinois on its eastern bluffs. There's a consensus amongst the hip-shaking, earth-quaking community that a 'Big One' is due before 2040. In 1990 the world's media descended on the settlement with TV crews and satellite dishes after rumours spread via telex agencies that the earth was about to shake, in what became known as the New Madrid Media Quake, one of the biggest non-news events in history.

The last couple of big ones struck with such a force the president was said to have felt the vibrations in the White House, hundreds of miles away. This was in the winter of 1811/12, when, of the 2,000 recorded tremors, five were believed to have galloped past what is now considered the feared 8 mark on the Richter scale. The strongest hit at a quarter past three on the morning of 7 February 1812 and is believed to have reached the dreaded 8.8, making it one of the strongest earthquakes on record, a quake that not only completely obliterated anything that was left of old New Madrid, but also caused the Mississippi river to run backwards to the north for several hours, and shot seismic balls of solidified petroleum into the air from fissures and crevices believed to have swallowed people whole in an instant. The Midwest and the Deep South continued developing at a wild pace as the seismic past faded away in the collective memory. Hugely developed cities like St Louis and Memphis now await a rude reminder of the Earth's hidden powers.

We steer our truck away from Highway 55 and weave our way in between the wooden one-storey buildings of New Madrid to find an empty parking lot behind the memorial library. Inside the white wood-panelled building we are greeted by two ladies in their sixties, Virginia Carlson and Marsha Hunter. We explain that we are looking for any traces of John Evans, based on what he shared with us in his 1797 letter to Samuel Jones, an extraordinary document of his travels in the West, which mentions that his hosts here were Azor Rees and his wife. They have never heard of John Evans but are familiar with the Rees name, and we are able to deduce from the records (Goodspeed's *History of Southeast Missouri*) that Evans would have stayed with his 'country people', Azor Rees and his wife, Dinah Martin, both of whom could claim some Welsh heritage.

We sit around a Formica table in a boiling-hot back room, fans whirring on the ceiling and a window wide open to let in a barely existent breeze, and get to work on a pile of books, census records and documents that the ladies have collected.

'Ah! Here's Azor Rees,' declares Virginia, finding his name in one of the records.

Marsha points east through the open window, towards the river. Both she and Virginia speculate that Azor's grave would long ago have fallen into the Mississippi with all the old cemeteries. We return to Evans's letter and are reminded of the grim reality of his situation here. Having left Samuel Jones's house in March with one dollar seventy-five, he had now spent all his funds on getting to this distant territory, which was about as west as anyone could hope to travel overland at this time.

Like sand, the Welsh got everywhere. New Madrid was even founded by one: William Morgan. Evans was fortunate to have located some compatriots in the land of the king of Spain, but it was here in New Madrid that John Evans faced his first major disaster. Ten days after his arrival, he was struck down with a violent fever, followed by delirium. Diagnosis: malaria.

Having reached New Madrid, roughly the halfway point on his journey to the supposed land of the Mandans, whom he hoped were indeed the Madogwys, his one-man expedition had stalled, seemingly indefinitely, due to a severe case of the dreaded chills, as malaria was commonly known. This could have killed him there and then, but for the intervention of Azor Rees's wife, who nursed him back to life.

Who was this woman who saved John Evans's life? Aside from romantic liaisons, speculated upon by dramatist Gareth Miles and the writer Emyr Jones, she is the most meaningful female character in Evans's documented travels.

'Here's the widow. See?' Marsha says, indicating a line in the census record. 'Dinah Martin.'

According to the archive, following Azor's death she married a Gray but divorced him for cruel treatment.

'Mrs Gray is mentioned here,' Marsha says, picking up Louis Houck's *The Spanish Regime in Missouri*, 'by Reverend Timothy Flint as "a woman of rare culture and learning".'

'Very interesting job, this: librarian,' Virginia enthuses.

'I can imagine,' I concur, nodding my head at 160 beats per minute.

'It says Azor Rees died in 1797,' adds Virginia. 'And had one daughter.'

'Oh, he did? He had a daughter!' says Marsha, delighted.

'That's a good thing,' nods Virginia.

'Yes, a wife and a daughter. Wait – he had a wife and a daughter and six slaves and nine cattle,' Marsha says, looking at the record, 'and 600 bushels of corn. That's what it says.'

I feel sick to the core. 'Azor Rees had six slaves?'

I ponder how Evans would have handled the fact that he was being nursed back to health in a slave-owning household. He was now in Spanish Louisiana and living under very different rules from those of his radical friends on the East Coast. Are these 'All the great people of this place' whom he refers to in his letter to Samuel Jones? They may well have nursed him back to life. Was he just desperately ill in his malarial stupor or had his morals collapsed? Either way, one imagines that his activist friend Morgan John Rhys would have been horrified.

'I have a friend named Anne Evans Copeland, but she doesn't think that she's any relation to John Evans,' continues Marsha. 'But she's got her own metal detector. She's out today looking for Civil War things – bullets and stuff.'

'So was this a strategic place during the Civil War as well?' I ask.

'Yes, we had a big battle right upstream from here,' Marsha says.

'What was the divide here?' I enquire, as the penny drops and I realize that I've finally reached the South.

'What was the divide?' Marsha laughs. 'Most of the people here were Confederates. I had three great-grandfathers who went off together to Memphis and enlisted in the army. Same day, same time. Three of them, which is kind of a coincidence, I think.'

'Yes, all of our ancestors came and stayed. Mine did. Mine came from Virginia,' adds Virginia, of all people.

'Mine didn't leave even after the earthquake. They stayed right here,' Marsha reveals.

'So was the whole town destroyed in the earthquake?' I say, beginning to worry.

'Pretty much,' Marsha states matter-of-factly.

'A few people did stay, but most left. It scared them to death,' says Virginia.

I ask them about the landscape John Evans would have traversed here 200 years ago.

'He would have seen a giant forest. Very, very thick trees, and then the rest of it over to the west of here was all swamp. The nickname for this area is Swamp East Missouri, instead of South East Missouri. They drained it in the mid 1930s and there are millions and millions of ditches, all interlaced. But before then it was just one big swamp. New Madrid was a high area here on the bank of the river, and that's why it was settled so early.'

It was Swamp East Missouri that created the perfect conditions for Evans's malaria.

I try to verify Evans's own description of his journey as contained in his correspondence, and wonder what the large river reptiles that he mentions might have been.

'Snakes?' guesses Virginia.

'Oh yes, we have snakes,' says Marsha. 'My husband went frog-gigging one time. Do you know what that is? You get a little boat and a long pole with a gig on the end of it – like a spear – and you float around in the streams at night with a flashlight, and when you hear a frog you shine a light on him and then stick him with that thing. They took my husband – he was from Minnesota, a Yankee – on a gig and a big old water moccasin got right out of the tree and into the boat. He said, "Never again" – that was the end of his frog-gigging. One trip. Those darn bullfrogs are about that big,' she says, her arms aloft. 'They're big. I mean, the leg on it is, you know, big.'

So Evans, unstoppable on his quest to track down the lost tribe, would have been walking the high, tree-lined banks along the Mississippi, sometimes submerged in the river itself and occasionally crawling slowly through undeveloped swampland full of large frogs, snakes, and even alligators (it's not far-fetched to imagine that these reptiles would have been as far north as this in the eighteenth century), as the war raged between the Osage tribe and the Spanish to the north and a malarial fever deranged his head.

'We're going to follow his route north to Kaskaskia tomorrow,' I tell the ladies.

'Kaskaskia? That's an island. It used to be a pretty busy place, but I don't know if there's hardly anything left on that old thing.' Marsha's assessment doesn't seem very promising.

Although Evans doesn't seem to have left much of a trace here, we have gained some distressing insights into the life of his hosts during his time in New Madrid in 1793. In turn I thank my own hosts for humouring me and my ignorant questions, but I'm still curious about one thing.

'Are there still earthquakes here?' I ask them.

'Yes, we still have them,' declares Virginia.

'We pay no attention to them,' says Marsha indifferently.

'Yes, you just get used to them,' smiles Virginia.

[You] Reached the Mississippi,
Took an oath in New Madrid,
Fell into a maiden's arms,
Malaria on your lips.

ELEVEN

NEW MADRID
TO
KASKASKIA

Lost in the infinite wilderness of America

After being bedridden for two long months at the Rees household, Evans declared that his 'resolution and anxiety for proceeding on my voyage [was] heightened to such a pitch that I was determined to risk my life feeble as I was . . .' Evans's ambition to locate the lost tribe could not be quelled even by a serious disease. One can imagine that the climate, both political and atmospheric, was unbearable for the cold-blooded northerner. However, to leave this safe haven in an attempt to walk 2,000 miles through war-torn swampland suggests that his fearless character bordered on the insane.

Now began one of the toughest physical endurance tests of his long journey. 'Oh! Unsufferable thirst and hunger is an amusement in comparison to this,' he commented, as he continued north along the Mississippi, still in a hallucinatory state and severely weakened by his fever, in the company of one man only.

By the end of the first day they had managed to veer off the ill-defined path that led to St Louis, and now Evans was walking through the wilderness, sometimes up to his neck in water and surrounded by 'the biggest water reptiles I ever saw'. A week into his journey, his clothes, hat and shoes had disintegrated and he was travelling virtually naked, complaining that the hostile sun was threatening 'to bake [his] brains like a cake'. He also became temporarily blinded. Having become too weak to continue, he rested for a day at the small settlement of Virgen before crossing back to the east side of the Mississippi to the booming village of Kaskaskia, in Illinois territory.

There his fever turned nervous and he complained of spending several days in a hallucinatory delirious state, being 'neither asleep nor awake'. Luckily for Evans, help was at hand and yet another Welsh family out on the wild frontier took him in and attempted to nurse him back to health.

This description of Evans's journey north along the western shore of the Mississippi River, taken from his letter to Samuel Jones, needs no further colour. We note the contrast between our journeys, particularly apparent as what takes us a couple of pleasant days in a truck obviously traumatized Evans to the core. This was the reality of travelling in the eighteenth century. In the late July heat of the Mississippi basin, it would have been hell. (That said, in a vaguely parallel if pathetic turn of events, a hitherto unknown allergy to one of the ingredients in my sunscreen has also caused me to go temporarily blind, whilst the unusually hot sun of this severest of droughts has burned my nose to the point where I'm wearing a Band-Aid on it.) Disorientatingly, the village of Kaskaskia has changed sides in more ways than one since Evans's day. When he left Virgen on the Spanish-controlled west side of the Mississippi, he crossed over to Kaskaskia in Illinois, back on the east bank, the US side. Since that time, facilitated by the dramatic seismic events of the nineteenth century, the Mississippi has changed course, as rivers do, ploughing into the furrow of the smaller Kaskaskia River and eventually turning the Kaskaskia peninsula into an island, firmly to the west side of today's river. Crucially, however, the old Missouri–Illinois state border has been maintained along the old river route, regardless of the fact that elsewhere the river defines the border. This will prove hugely significant for our journey later on.

Much as it has changed sides geographically, Kaskaskia has also had a turbulent political past. The old peninsular village of Evans's day was for the most part washed away by the Mississippi, and the island now boasts a modest population of fourteen. Its name alludes to its past as a significant Illini tribal village. This in turn attracted a French Jesuit mission, and the village then developed into a trading post and garrison. It became the capital of French-controlled Upper Louisiana, prompting King Louis XV in 1741 to present its church with a bell cast in France. It soon fell to the British and became part of Quebec. The church bell was chimed by American soldiers, including one John Rice Jones, in 1778 when they took the town from the British during the American Revolution, and the bell was renamed the Liberty Bell of the West. Kaskaskia was then briefly, in its heyday, the state capital of Illinois. That same bell still rings in Kaskaskia. And even though a lot has changed, we can accurately say that we have heard the same bell ringing that John Evans would have heard in July 1793 when he stumbled, broken, into town.

It's extraordinary how Evans, travelling through the far reaches of western America, was running into Welsh people everywhere. After his ass was saved by Azor Rees in New Madrid, in Kaskaskia he was taken in by another Welsh family. That same former American soldier John Rice Jones had left Gwynedd to join the American Revolution and had brought his family wholesale to this multicultural village in the Illinois, and Evans would have found in him a radical Welsh-speaking compatriot. This fortuitous meeting perhaps explains why Evans settled here for so long as he recuperated from malaria and awaited his next opportunity to push on with his Madogwys expedition.

New experiences were coming thick and fast for him. Here in Kaskaskia he would have met French, First Nation Americans and mixed-race fur trappers. The latter regularly ran errands up the lower reaches of the Missouri, where they trapped river animals and traded within an ancient network of Native American routes that had moved goods on a continental basis for centuries before the European invasion. These hardy individuals, for the most part French-speakers, were exploring areas never seen by the colonial armies, but they were out for themselves. They weren't surveying the land and they had no political or imperial ambitions to oust their tribal hosts. Many married into the tribes and their children became crucial interpreters between these very different cultures. They would bring back furs for men like John Rice Jones, a lawyer who acted as an agent and attorney for a large Canadian fur-trading firm, the House of Todd. This was a significant connection for Evans to have stumbled upon in his bid to get to the upper reaches of the Missouri, and the advice of the trappers would have been enlightening, mentally preparing him for the realities of the next stage of the journey.

ESCAPE FROM KASKASKIA

We now cross over the Mississippi from the east side at a town called Chester, where E. C. Segar, the illustrator and creator of Popeye, was born, and drive upstream before crossing a smaller bridge over a creek on to Kaskaskia island itself.

It's a beautiful place, with lush open farmland cut through with straight tree-lined roads that somehow look French, and clouds of summer dust which blow in from the shore. The old town grid remains rigidly in place, and a monumental Catholic church belies its current status as the second-least-populated incorporated settlement in the state of Illinois. The local cemetery has far more residents than the town itself.

We engender some curious looks from guarded well-wishers who come to inspect John and the truck. One of them has even heard of John Evans. A second, highly perceptive man is so painfully aware that he looks like a generic small-town hillbilly that he refuses to be photographed as he thinks I would exploit his image for this very reason (to my shame I probably would). Wearing a baseball cap, a dirty vest which exposes his belly, and oversized jeans, he is nevertheless welcoming enough to bring out a six-pack of beer from his pickup and settle in for a long conversation. We bring more food and beer from our truck, start building some sandwiches and crack open the ales.

Suddenly, after three or four cans of Blue Ribbon each, the mood changes and our friend's gregarious personality darkens as he starts vociferously to contest not only our John Evans story but also our reluctance now to continue into the third six-pack that he's retrieved from the orange pickup.

Fearing that the next thing out of the pickup will be a gun, cool-headed John for once leads the charge, forcing me with an iron will to return him to the truck. Being in no fit state to drive, I let John take the wheel for the first time. We screech out of what you could describe as the village green, in front of the bell tower, but as John attempts the first right turn he doesn't see the street sign and crashes into it. I jump out to assess any damage, but before I can make out anything in these last minutes of dusk, John commands in a booming voice I haven't heard before, 'Get back into the chariot, NOW!' He also barks out a tirade of frankly unprintable coarse adjectives in his roughest Welsh, and I begin to understand his urgency.

Blue Ribbon Man has followed us in his pickup and is now ranting outside as he approaches the truck cabin. Once again John stamps his felt foot hard on the accelerator and the gigantic wheels of the truck charge up the unpaved road, leaving a blizzard of dust and a destroyed street sign behind us. John, aware of his felony and worried that Blue Ribbon Man has phoned the cops, realizes that at this point we should truly applaud the Gods of the Mississippi River's dramatic 1881 decision to flood the valley and seek another route beyond Kaskaskia, as it means that we now have a state line we can cross within five miles, *without* having to cross the famous river.

HEEEEEEEOOOOOOOOOOOOOOO! John hoots the truck's horn, and we head towards the Missouri state line, faster than the wind, when, alas! Like a gigantic mosquito in the rear-view mirror the orange headlights of a familiar pickup loom: Blue Ribbon Man is catching up fast behind us. We calculate that we can probably still make the five miles across the island to the state line and the anonymity of Highway 55 when, goddamn it, hasn't our beer-can friend just arranged for a second pickup to try (in our minds at least) to stall our journey, as from a side road, cutting in front of us, comes another set of wheels out of the darkness. Now zooming down a rural track at full throttle, forming the filling in a giant metal sandwich that consists of a large black truck between two rusty pickups, I start to regret ever embarking on this journey. Gripped by a tense paranoia, I reflect on my life so far, as the vehicle in front tries to slow down our passage and Blue Ribbon Man starts bumping into the bumper.

Thankfully, we are able to contain this cold war up to the modest bridge that crosses the creek where once flowed America's longest river. There's no sign of Illinois cops, and we are now out of their jurisdiction and able to snake back on to Highway 55, which leads us eventually to the safety of our own gated fort, the downtown St Louis Recreational Vehicle Park.

Up to St Louis,
Kaskaskia on the way,
Walking through the wilderness,
Sicker by the day,
Imaginary volcanoes,
And reptiles crawl around,
Your mind was baked just like a cake,
As trouble gathered round.

TWELVE

ST LOUIS
AND
THE INCARCERATION
OF
JOHN EVANS

After a year and a half of lying low in Kaskaskia, the chameleon John Evans, now in seemingly full health, had become an active Freemason, well connected to prominent fur traders and government officials in both Kaskaskia and Cahokia, an American settlement further north up the Mississippi that had been founded next to the biggest known grouping of prehistoric Native American ceremonial mounds (the American equivalent in terms of scale and mystery to Stonehenge in England).

It was from Cahokia that in December 1794 Evans caught wind of a three-year expedition that the Spanish-government-sponsored Missouri Company was planning up the then largely unexplored Missouri basin, beyond which they hoped lay the Pacific Ocean. With ambitions to find work on this voyage, which would take him to the heartlands of the Madogwys, Evans declared 'Now or never' and defected once more over the Mississippi back into Spanish territory at St Louis. But whereas New Madrid, having been founded by Mr Morgan the Welshman, was a safe haven within New Spain for Americans, St Louis was an altogether different proposition: a French-speaking settlement, governed from a distance by the Spanish capital at New Orleans, it was at that point on code red, fearing an imminent attack from the hostile mercenary forces of the rampaging General George Rodgers Clark across the river.

His friends despaired of Evans's impulsive designs; indeed Morgan John Rhys wrote in a letter to William Owen Pughe that Evans 'had not a sufficient knowledge of mankind to balance his enterprising enthusiasm'. Fully aware of the dangers he faced, the fearless Don

Juan crossed the freezing river regardless and was immediately arrested, on suspicion of being a US spy. Unable to speak French and with the fanciful story regarding a Welsh tribe his only line of defence, he was 'loaded with Iron and put in the stoks [*sic*]' in the cruel cold of the St Louis winter.

By contrast, when we arrive in St Louis in late August it's boiling hot, and after showers at the RV Park we head into town to meet the historian Carolyn Gilman at 4th and Walnut.

A Journey Back in Time

with
Carolyn Gilman
at
the 4th and Walnut Multistory [typo!] Car Park

Now in 3-D!

'Well, we're standing right on the site of the original fort,' says Gilman. 'The fort would actually have stood on that intersection and spanned this street, but at the south-west corner of the fort was the dungeon where they kept political prisoners. And that would have been right where we're standing right now. So that's almost certainly where John Evans would have been kept when he was thrown in jail after he arrived . . .'

I turn my head and look down the street. Eero Saarinen's famous mid-century Gateway Arch towers ahead in a graceful arc, but Gilman has a vivid imagination when recreating the past. In her presence the buildings that are here today are erased on command by her hand gestures, and although it will take me a few minutes to adjust to her descriptive CGI powers, I get there eventually – and John, well, John's seen it all before so we've placed him behind the bars of a multi-storey car-park window in the exact location that he was jailed the first time around.

'Oh, I wish they had done some archaeology before they put this thing up,' declares Gilman, tut-tutting the whole grey high-rise car-park structure as if it's a clumsy though well-meaning elephant. 'It was the dead of winter when he was thrown into the dungeon, and it would have been very cold. He was suspected of being an American spy because he'd come from across the river. There was great tension here at the time between the Spanish, who were on the west side of the river, and the Americans, who were on the east side. And when Evans crossed the river and showed up in St Louis from the east side, he was immediately suspected of being up to no good.'

I wonder aloud what physical condition Evans would have been in, and whether his malaria would have recurred in the hellish dungeon conditions.

'Everybody got malaria who came here,' responds Gilman. 'It was absolutely endemic in the Mississippi Valley. It's not that malaria couldn't happen here today, it's that the Anopheles mosquitoes that carry it were basically wiped out when they drained the country, channelled the river and made farmland out of swamps. They called it *la maladie du pays*. It was the disease of the country because it was so common here, and that's why the Indians from up the Missouri River, the Mandan and other northern Indians, didn't want to come down to St Louis – because they were afraid of catching it,' she explains.

Standing atop the slight hill where the car-park building rests and the fortification wall of the city used to stand, we now look east and imagine what John would have seen over two centuries ago. A new church stands on the site of the original one that John would have viewed behind the stockades, but the same Mississippi flows behind it, and we ponder whether Evans could ever have imagined the concrete slabs of today's city.

St Louis was founded in 1764 by a group of French settlers, following the French defeat by the British at the close of the 1763 French and Indian War, which led to France's exit from North America. Everything east of the Mississippi, including the settled French lands of the Illinois, now fell under British control, whilst everything to the west of the river was ceded to the Spanish. The French settlers of the Illinois would have faced an existential predicament: should they stay put and become British subjects? For some this was an unpalatable option, and they chose instead to flee over the Mississippi to Spanish-controlled territory – perhaps, they thought, the lesser of two evils.

Those who chose Spanish citizenship on the west of the river built a town unlike any found on the anglicized East Coast. Based on the classic French Illinois ground plan, it would have consisted of fenced-in stockade houses with a vertical-post construction and wide porches for the hot summers. Apart from the taverns, there would have been no American-style shopfronts. All the houses and traders were hidden within their own walled agricultural realms, consisting of a house, garden and barn or whatever they needed for their particular calling. There were no signs. Everything happened behind closed doors, so you had to know where to go. The Illinois region at this time resembled medieval France, with French-speaking hamlets composed of farms, churches and mills, connected by a network of roads. The new settlement strived to retain that culture, and resented any interference from the Spanish government in New Orleans.

'The French who settled here were an uppity bunch,' explains Gilman. 'They gave the Spanish who came to supposedly rule them a hard time. As a matter of fact the first Spanish commandant who came up the river to establish Spanish authority here in St Louis got kicked out by the local populace and had to go back down to New Orleans. So after that they sent up a Frenchman to rule St Louis, because they knew that the French would accept other Frenchmen. The person in charge when John Evans got here was Trudeau, who was a Frenchman working for Spain. Then Evans comes to St Louis and he hooks up with Jacques Clamorgan, who is also Welsh. And it's really extraordinary that there were all these Welsh people out there who were hanging together and sticking up for Evans whenever he got in trouble, because he seems to have gotten in trouble quite a lot.'

'Yeah, he had a very eventful journey,' I agree. I feel like a broken man and we've only been travelling for two weeks. I'm sunburnt and we've been sleeping in RV parks; by John Evans's standards this would be an absolute luxury, but still, I'm feeling pretty rough.

It's difficult for me to comprehend the impossible suffering faced by Evans. He was jailed for what we assume was only a few months in early 1795, but the winters in St Louis in the late eighteenth century were incredibly harsh and it would have been tough going. In comparison to the chains of the cold dark dungeon in the Spanish fort, his periods as an exhibit in the stocks at the square in front of the church would have seemed like light relief. The entire population of the 2,500-strong settlement must have seen him there and wondered where the hell he had come from.

Luckily, as it turned out, it was so cold that it was likely the Mississippi River had frozen over. Judge George Turner, a highly regarded acquaintance of Evans from Kaskaskia, was on good terms with Trudeau, the French-speaking governor at St Louis, and presumably walked across the river and interceded on Evans's behalf, corroborating his story that he was in fact on the trail of a lost Welsh tribe. Now with the cautious backing of the ever-suspicious Trudeau, Evans fell in with a charismatic Caribbean man of Welsh heritage, Jacques Clamorgan, one of the main players of the Missouri Company, the trading firm that aimed to open up the vast lands that lay beyond St Louis. In the meantime Evans may have experienced other joys at his new francophone boom-village.

'They held a lot of balls and parties and dances in St Louis; it was a very convivial town, according to everybody who visited here. But you had to be invited, of course. I'm sure that Evans would have been invited. Strangers were always sought after because they were novel, and somebody with a story as dramatic as Evans's would have been invited to parties. Especially if he knew Jacques Clamorgan, because Clamorgan was one of the richest people in town. He's famous today because he had an interracial marriage – he was married to an African lady – and so he was an iconoclast, a man who followed the beat of his own drum. He flouted convention.'

Evans had landed on his feet again, but this time in a very different, Catholic, French-speaking world. He would have been unable to practise his Protestant faith, except in his own bedroom, as Catholicism was 'the only show in town', Gilman explains. He had gone through yet another transformation. Governor Trudeau now furnished him with a trilingual passport as a citizen of Spanish Louisiana. In the French section, the latest incarnation of the ever-transforming Welshman: Monsieur Jean Evans.

ACT TWO, PART TWO
A LEFT TURN AT ST LOUIS

CHARTING THE MISSOURI BASIN

PRINCIPAL CHARACTERS

THE MISSOURI RIVER

The most twisting river in America, and if you look at it from a certain perspective, and are prone to exaggeration, the longest river in the world.

LIEUTENANT GOVERNOR ZENON TRUDEAU

Eighteenth-century governor of Upper Louisiana – the French-speaking enclave of Spanish Louisiana – and commandant of St Louis.

JACQUES CLAMORGAN

Eighteenth-century, St Louis-based Welshman of Caribbean extraction; director of the Missouri Company.

COMMANDANT JAMES 'SANTIAGO' MACKAY

Scottish general working for Spain, who guides Evans halfway towards the lost tribe of the Madogwys.

KLIPH SCURLOCK

Drummer for The Flaming Lips, and leading American Welshophile.

W. RAYMOND WOOD

The US's leading academic on John Evans.

CHIEF BLACKBIRD

Eighteenth-century formidable chief of the Omaha nation.

DENNIS HASTINGS

Present-day UMO^{n}HO^n activist.

CHIEF BLACK CAT

Eighteenth-century first chief of the Mandan villages.

CHIEF SHEHEKE

Also known as Big White; eighteenth-century second chief of the Mandan villages.

CORY SPOTTED BEAR

Present-day Mandan warrior.

EDWIN BENSON

The only living first-language speaker of the Mandan language.

MARILIN HUDSON

Present-day museum curator.

KEITH BEAR

Present-day Mandan flute player and storyteller.

CALVIN GRINELL

Present-day Tribal Historic Preservation Officer at the Fort Berthold Reservation.

ONE

THE MISSOURI RIVER,
AKA
THE BIG MUDDY

Fast track to the Madogwys

It's impossible to fathom the excitement that Evans would have felt in his bones. He was now two and a half eventful years into his journey, accepted in St Louis, the town located at the confluence of the Mississippi River and the great Missouri River, and it was a thousand miles or so up this very river that he expected to find his glorious prize: the Madogwys. Trudeau, the governor at St Louis, would remain highly suspicious of Evans till the end, but was persuaded by Judge Turner of the potential advantages direct communication with the lost Welsh tribe would bring to St Louis. Having freed him from jail, Trudeau gave Evans the green light to travel up the Missouri, and was likely to have made him aware of a 2,000-peso reward for anyone who reached the Pacific. As Evans had no resources to his name, he hedged his bets on finding work on the Missouri Company expedition that would set sail in September. By March he was safely back in Cahokia, staying at the house of a Mr Arundel and awaiting his opportunity to head north.

The imperial-sized Missouri Company trade expedition hoped to break the river blockades of the Otto, Ponca and Omaha tribes in the southern part of the river and those of the Lakota (Sioux) and Sahnish (Arikara) tribes to the north. Building a fort at each tribal area would enable them to maintain a direct trade route with the Mandan and Hidatsa tribes to the north, secure the northern border of the Spanish empire and eject the British traders who had come down from Canada and built a trading post at the Mandan villages. Furthermore, they would use this Mandan base to facilitate their ultimate ambition: to secure a route to the Pacific Ocean and make that first cross-continental journey.

Of course, Europeans thought that land could be owned, but that the rivers were free-for-all channels of transportation. The tribes thought the exact opposite: land could not be owned, but rivers? By all means! The rivers belonged to the tribes through whose territories they flowed. It was a tribe's right to control the commerce on their rivers, and like any modern nation they did this by means of tariffs and tolls. It wasn't in the interest of any tribe to let Spanish traders sell a boatload of guns to a rival nation upriver, for example. When the colonial powers were carving up the map of America, they were essentially claiming trading rights to those areas rather than full-blown sovereignty, fully aware that these vast lands were still controlled on the ground by the original nation tribes with whom they now sought partnerships, trading rights on their goods and land to build forts. Unfortunately for the great nations of the northern plains, this potentially cordial understanding of sovereignty was not to last.

The Missouri Company was headed by the lieutenant governor of Upper Louisiana, Don Zenon Trudeau, and Jacques Clamorgan, the enterprising Caribbean Welshman. The company had already suffered two previous failed expeditions up the Missouri, and the leader of the second expedition, Jean Baptiste Truteau (not to be mistaken for Zenon Trudeau, governor of St Louis), was still stranded upriver, having failed in his attempt to reach the Mandan nation. But now they had decided to attempt a third expedition on a scale that was unknown in these waters. Clamorgan had made a pact with Andrew Todd, a Canada-based trader known to John Rice Jones in Kaskaskia. Given the support of the Spanish government, Todd had agreed to move his enterprise to New Orleans and provide huge investment to the company over the three-year period that a journey to the Pacific and back would presumably take.

All Evans needed to do now was to persuade the Spanish to take him with them. But how was he to convince them he was fit for a role on a professional river expedition? He had no experience of the cold waters of the Missouri, unlike most of the men in St Louis, who were seasoned river-men, trappers and hunters. His surveying skills may have been known to Clamorgan and Governor Trudeau, as was certainly his unusual story regarding the Welsh tribe, but why risk an unknown quantity only recently converted to the Spanish cause on a major expansionist enterprise? By sheer chance, luck now came Evans's way by means of an unlikely encounter between a Welshman and a Scotsman, 300 long miles away in Cincinnati.

CONCERT AT THE CONTEMPORARY ART MUSEUM, ST LOUIS

It's been a busy morning walking around multi-storey car parks and time-travelling with Carolyn Gilman. In the afternoon I play five new songs about Evans's adventure as a session at the KDHX radio station, then we finally head to the Contemporary Art Museum to set up for a show. It's a brutal yet beautiful concrete building by the Allied Works architecture firm, with an airy warren of performance spaces that makes playing a show all the more exciting. Better still, Kliph Scurlock, an American Welshophile and member of The Flaming Lips, has joined John and me for a few days, to play the drums. His friends, Jess and Doug, both sporting sunglasses, have come along too for a road trip from their home in Lawrence, Kansas. We reinvent the show: the DVD of Gwyn A. Williams's Welsh-ploitation documentary on Madog (the opening act) has suffered some kind of scratch and it's distorting like hell, but in the context of a museum gallery space the audience are open to anything so they go with it, then we bombard them with a heavy set, now with LOUD drums. In addition, we introduce a video-game section to the show, where we provide a live soundtrack to volunteers who offer their services to play the game *Whale Trail* on our big video screen. How times have changed in St L.

In the end we abandon the stage and walk the songs through the museum spaces, followed by the audience. We end the night singing songs outside the concrete spaceship in the open air, the night stars shimmering along to the music just as they would have done a couple of centuries past.

TWO

IN CELEBRATION

*Of a fortuitous meeting between Morgan John Rhys
and Commandant James 'Santiago' Mackay at
Cincinnati, which facilitates the passage of John Evans
up the Missouri River towards his ultimate goal, the
discovery of the Madogwys*

The fact that there was a second politically revolutionary Welsh-man weaving his way through the American West at exactly the same time that John Evans was there was to be of the utmost value to him. Unbeknownst to him, Morgan John Rhys had reached Cincinnati after his anti-slavery crusade through the Southern states and was to provide Evans with a vital supporting role.

Meanwhile, Jacques Clamorgan and Governor Trudeau had managed to persuade General James Mackay, a formidable Scottish adventurer who had made far-reaching inroads into the Canadian West as a British subject, to defect to the Spanish side and settle in St Louis. Mackay was disgruntled by his treatment and disappointing rewards at the hands of the North West Company, Hudson Bay Company and renegade fur trader Donald Mackay, having been a valuable asset to all three. In Clamorgan's offer he saw an opportunity to earn significant tracts of land from his new sponsors, and after many years in the cold wilderness he must have jumped at the chance.

Clamorgan had secretly asked General Mackay to lead his new three-year expedition to the Mandan nation and the Pacific Ocean beyond, and he was undoubtedly more than qualified for the role. In 1787 he had visited the Mandans from the north, through Canada, and was the first European to provide significant written documentation of the Mandan tribe at their Knife River villages. The first European documentation of the Mandans at their original Heart River site was by Pierre Gaultier de Varennes, sieur de La Vérendrye, who reached them in 1738. However, without speaking the language, neither Mackay nor Vérendrye had been able to verify whether the Mandans had any connection to the Welsh, though Vérendrye had furthered the myth of a pale-skinned tribe, which was interpreted by the ever-hopeful Welsh as a sighting of the Madogwys themselves. What was particularly audacious about this new expedition was the hope to reach the Mandans from the south and maintain Louisiana's grip on trade up to the 49th parallel.

In July 1795 General Mackay was on a journey back from New York when he had a chance meeting with the one and only Morgan John Rhys in Cincinnati. Mackay recalls in a journal that he eventually passed on to William Clark:

On my way from New York to Louisiana I met a worthy Gentleman, Dr Jn Rees, whom after informing him of my intended expedition, furnished me with a small vocabulary of the Welch language written by himself and informed me respecting a Mr John Evans from Wales who was gone to Illinois with the intention of traveling westward to see the supposed Welch tribe.

Furthermore, he also believed in 'the possibility of their existence and considering the light such a discovery might throw on the history of America [I] was determined to use all the means in my power to unveil the mystery'. With this in mind, he goes into action: 'Having arrived in Louisiana, I got ready for my voyage to the West. I sent for, & engaged for my assistant, Mr Evans who spoke & wrote the Welch language with facility.'

Evans had got the job! By the end of August he was now second in command on the biggest Spanish expedition ever assembled in Louisiana. It sounds like a joke: here were a Scotsman and a Welshman employed by the Spanish king, leading a boat full of French-speakers into the precarious tribal waters of the Missouri River.

W. Raymond Wood, the great scholar and archaeologist of the Missouri, has observed in his masterpiece, *Prologue to Lewis and Clark* (2003), the likelihood that the Mackay–Evans party would have started their river journey not from St Louis but from St Charles, then the most westerly European settlement on the Missouri. By travelling the twenty-five miles between the settlements overland, they would have bypassed the hazards and rapids of the confluence of the Mississippi and Missouri rivers that lay just north of St Louis.

It's likely that they left on 1 September 1795 in four vessels. A mixture of barge-like keelboats known as 'berchas' and large canoe-shaped river craft known as 'pirogues' made up the flotilla. Clamorgan noted that there was a boatload of gifts and trade goods for each of the Mandan, Arikara and Sioux tribes and that the fourth boatload contained supplies to fuel the expedition to its supposed destination: the Pacific Ocean. The only slight problem was that nobody fully knew what lay between St Charles and the West Coast.

As second in command, Evans would have commandeered his own boat. The crew consisted of thirty men, so not far off in scale and ambition from Meriwether Lewis and William Clark's Corps of Discovery expedition, which had the same destination in mind when it left nearly a decade later with a crew of thirty-two men (plus Seaman the dog).

Mackay and Evans's crew would have been allocated a portion of hard liquor at least twice a day and would have breakfasted on a dried-maize porridge called hominy. Lard and biscuits would have been served for lunch, and wild game and deer hunted during the day on the riverbank for dinner. As it was quicker to walk than row against the current, the boats would have been pulled along from the shore when possible. The journey would have been very slow.

When Professor George Miles, Curator of Maps at Yale's Beinecke Library, spoke to me after one of the shows, he captured the exhilaration that the young explorers must have felt: 'Well, it's a romantic history, it's an extraordinary adventure to travel beyond the bounds of most people's experience. And to do it among people whose languages and cultures were just beginning to be understood, I can't imagine how exciting it must have been, and a lot of people will make comparisons between travelling in the West and the idea of space travel. It was like going to another world; it was leaving behind all that you knew.'

ST CHARLES

John, Kliph, Doug and I nose the bus into the quaint village centre of St Charles, which is all French and fancy for North America. Jess has driven the car back to Lawrence, Kansas, and Doug (who's yet to take off his sunglasses) has agreed to drive the truck for a few days. The roads are narrow, and we have to be careful not to scratch the paint of the colourful colonial exteriors. We're heading for the Lewis and Clark Expedition Museum, where a few of the volunteers who in 2004 undertook a transcontinental bicentennial re-enactment of the Corps's journey have agreed to let us try some of the vessels they took out on the journey. Given that the Lewis and Clark expedition set out only nine years after Evans, the technology of their boats would have been very similar, so this is our chance to try out a bercha and a pirogue for ourselves.

We opt for the pirogue first. John sits up front with a telescope whilst I take the rear. Kliph and Doug take photos from the bank. Nothing could have prepared me for the power of the river current. It's clearly lethal. In John Evans's day, before the Missouri's flow was controlled by man-made channels and a series of gigantic and often controversial river dams, the current would have been slower and so much easier to row against, although he would have faced an unpredictable barrage of hazards such as waterfalls, rapids, stray tree trunks and shallow banks and so, as mentioned above, it would have been easier and faster for the most part to walk the boat along the bank using a rope. Later, we try out a forty-foot keelboat that would have been able to carry a great deal of cargo even in the shallow waters of the Missouri. According to the volunteers, even a fully laden boat of this size could easily be walked upriver by only one person, leaving other expedition members free not only to hunt and forage, but also to document and survey the river and the surrounding landscape.

Although St Charles was the last European settlement on this journey and the interior beyond would have been mysterious, the crew was in all probability made up of French American and mixed-race Native American fur trappers or *voyageurs* (boatmen) with a knowledge of at least the lower portions of the Missouri River. It seems they made good early progress, completing the first stage from St Charles to the Platte River in today's Nebraska in forty-four days, so averaging fifteen miles a day (in comparison, Lewis and Clark took sixty days), a very healthy pace for such a flotilla. This means that they were unlikely to have been held up by any major setbacks, although Mackay in his journals does mention that the weather was 'bad' and that they were delayed by a pirogue that constantly filled with water. It would have been arduous work navigating, rowing, punting and pulling these boats upriver. A constant cloud of mosquitoes and blistering sunshine would have exacerbated the itch of the humidity.

Yet the journey would have been peaceful and, one imagines, beautiful as they travelled through the pristine landscape of cottonwood and elm, with only an abundance of wildlife for company and no sign of the feared Osage and Kansa nations, who roamed this region of the southern Missouri.

THREE

A RIVER JOURNEY THROUGH MISSOURI, THE SHOW-ME STATE

After our brief encounter with the boats in St Charles, we feel inclined to sample river travel for ourselves. The next show has been scheduled for an outdoor stage by the side of the Missouri River at Les Bourgeois Vineyards, near the seat of the University of Missouri at Columbia. So it actually seems easier to get there by river. It would take at least a week by bercha but only a couple of days by motorboat, so we settle for that. With 125 miles to go, we load John, Kliph Scurlock, a drum kit, a guitar, a tent and a bunch of cable into the boat, leaving cute St Charles behind us as we head into the interior.

Roaring upriver, Kliph and I take turns steering and napping as John again sits upfront, navigating. We hang a line behind us on the off chance that we might catch a catfish, although all we see are flying Japanese carp, which narrowly miss our heads as they jump and whizz over the boat. We've heard of a sandbank that's remained intact all summer at a bend upriver in Marin County. As we head to it, the drone of the motor becomes familiar after a while and we compose new songs, harmonizing to the drone, as Kliph hits beats on the side of the boat. We discuss recording an album, maybe when we get to Omaha. There's a steady stream of river traffic: the odd dredger, gravel barges, canoeing tourists, fishermen and fisherwomen. Trains toot by on the southern shore when the tracks run parallel to the riverbank.

We don't make it to Marin County, but we do find a solid sandbank on a turn in the river and set up camp, foraging for kindling on the shore. At this point a canoeist comes into view and shouts over at us, rowing with the current at quite a pace. He approaches quickly and comes to an abrupt stop on our little bank. John uncharacteristically calls him a 'river bum' out loud. It's highly embarrassing, but the guy understands – seeing how old John is, and how guys his age can get pretty moody on occasion. The stranger in the straw hat is sunburnt and thin and looks like he's already been on quite a journey.

'Do you mind if I join you here by the fire for a while?' he calls out.

'Sure,' we say, and help him to pull his canoe firmly to the sandy shore, where he stumbles out, his Bambi legs unfamiliar with dry land.

He has quite a story. Things hadn't been going too well for him in Omaha, where he was living, so he decided, whilst drunk in a bar, that he would clean himself up and canoe down to New Orleans in the Gulf of Mexico. Oh, only 1,200 miles or so! He is now over 300 miles into his journey, but the Missouri is a long old river. In fact, as Gwyn Williams once pointed out, if you include the remaining part of the Mississippi that it flows into in St Louis, it's actually the longest river on Earth.

We see two large catfish glistening in the bottom of his canoe. He pulls them out, along with two dagger-sized knives, as befits a man of the wilderness.

'You guys got any flour or anything?' he asks us.

We burrow into our supplies and pull out some eggs, oil and cornmeal. He digs out a large pan and a couple of pots of seasoning.

'Awl right!' he cries. 'We're gonna have quite a feast here.'

He has a kind of charming yet almost demonic enthusiasm, and his foraging skills are unparalleled. Out of a cloth bag he produces the tartest of wild grapes, juicy elderberries, wild nettles, oyster mushrooms, coral mushrooms, and cattail roots, which he tells us are 'better than mashed potatoes'. His diet variously includes wild game, catfish, squirrels and pigeons, and although he's never eaten one he's even caught a few turtles (he puts them back). He also has a bucket of tinned food as emergency rations.

We continue to shuffle through our combined food supplies, then we prepare to cook for the night.

A RECIPE FOR DISASTER: RIVER-CAUGHT CATFISH (OR PAN-FRIED CATTAILS IF YOU DON'T EAT MEAT)

Serves a small boatful (4 in this instance)

oil
a small ceremonial mound of cornmeal or flour
a palmful of paprika
a pinch of chopped fresh rosemary
a swoosh of garlic salt
3 pinches of black pepper
a pinch of white pepper
½ a discarded bird's skull of chilli powder
a favourite song or album, preferably long and monotonous
1 egg (chicken eggs are fine)

2 gulps of fine India Pale Ale
a shot of mezcal
2–3 garlic cloves, chopped
1 onion
4 catfish fillets or cattail roots

- Heat some oil in a pan. Throw the flour, paprika, rosemary, garlic salt, black and white pepper and chilli powder into a bowl and shake your head casually to the music, like you're not that interested (belying the fact you really are). Crack egg into second bowl. Pour in India Pale Ale and mezcal and mix.

- Chop the garlic and let it sweat in the pan. If you're using cattails, let them sweat for a while in the pan too. When the garlic is luminous and sweating, throw in the chopped onion. Stir it about and continue nodding head to the music.

- Dip the catfish or cattails in the egg and booze mixture until smothered and submerged. Throw them into the bowl of seasoning and mix around till they're completely covered, then put them in the pan to fry. When these are brown and crisp, serve on a bed of sorrow and dried Missouri mud.

- For special effect: smoke some weed and leave large knives lying around for extra paranoia.*

The food is delicious. The fire is a crackling furnace of a thousand TV sets at a pulsating, miniature discotheque. Our new-found friend,

* Weed is illegal in some countries and states, as are large knives.

Matthew, is a little drunk, and his stories are candid and wild and we are slightly scared.

He's eyed up our beers: special strength IPAs. 'Oh man, I've given up the beers, but they sure look good. It's thirsty work on that river.'

It seems that we're in for a long night with our new friend. With very little encouragement, he begins to fill out his story.

His full name is Matthew Batten. He'd lived in Omaha for a couple of years, trying to find a better job or get back to school, but things didn't quite work out. So, tired of the degradation of living midtown, and gang fights on the parking lot of the gas station where he worked nights, he and a friend decided, on a whim, whilst drinking in a bar, that they would commandeer a canoe and row down the Missouri to the Mississippi and on down to the Gulf of Mexico. He fell out with his friend in the meantime and continued planning alone.

It dawns on me that Matthew is in a way a modern-day John Evans, defying the odds stacked against him and following his own idiosyncratic route, albeit *down*river.

'I started on July 4th, Independence Day,' he begins. 'I thought that was an excellent idea, and it was really interesting the first day. People were having a baptism out there on the Oakhorn River, and I've never been a go-to-church-every-day kind of guy. I've been baptized before, I am Christian, but I thought it was an excellent idea to be baptized again before I started the trip, and I think it's brought me a lot of good luck.' A new beer is opened and drunk.

'I hope to learn a little bit about myself that I'd forgotten. I've been so caught up on the hustle and bustle of making it in this world, making a career, a good reputation, that I've forgotten what it's like to be out with nature, to just be who you are. I hope to learn a little bit more about the world around me and myself – that's what I hope to learn.'

The longer he talks, the more philosophical he gets. 'Right now, America is corporate-driven,' Matthew explains, IPA in one hand, knife in the other. 'If you have enough money, you can make any law you want to at this point. It will be a slow change, but the throw-everything-away, live-on-fast-food idealism is slowly coming to a stop. You've got this green movement going on right now, people growing their own gardens, and it's just starting.'

We are now enjoying the effects of multiple beers, and Kliph, who prefers not to drink, retreats to the tent as Matthew begins to reveal the darker side of river life: 'Like in Kansas City, I ran across this homeless camp and they invited me to stay with them. There was a camp of probably about forty people and ... Tyler, he's the guy who had his particular camp. One day Tyler wanted me to go panhandling with him. I'd never done it before, so I gave it a shot, made fourteen bucks. When we came back to camp, they were sitting around playing cards. Tyler had his knife out and I was sitting next to him, and I went over to some other friends and started playing cards with them. He starts getting really belligerent and angry with me and grabs his knife. Apparently nobody ever told him not to take a knife to a machete fight. I went over and grabbed my machete and said, "I think it's time for me to leave."'

After a long silence, unable to better Matthew's anecdote, I change the subject by talking about John Evans's journey upriver, like a Matthew in reverse, but by this point, beers downed, fire burning a layer off the skin of my face, I can't remember whether I've explained his story already, as Matthew already seems to know all about him.

'John Evans was really the first one to map the Missouri. He was travelling around America looking for a Welsh-speaking tribe of people. I guess he was this real loony. It was a lot more treacherous around then. They had these humungous logjams, for example, that would almost block the river.'

'So this river was totally different in 1795?' I ask, hazily imagining the logs from some film (possibly a horror) I'd seen on TV.

'Oh, completely different. Now you just see this large body of fairly calm-looking water moving along. Just a few miles up the river, back then it was a major rapid and it was so bad that they couldn't even take their boats down it, so they'd walk along the bank and slowly guide their canoe through the rapids.

'John Evans kind of set the standard, I believe. He didn't have maps, he didn't know what kind of tribes he would run into. There were tribes all over America; some of them were friendly, some of them were just warring tribes. Meeting with these people was really quite extraordinary. He didn't know what he was going to run into.'

I ask Matthew if it was a crazy journey for Evans to have taken.

'Oh, good God, yeah. Going against the current of the Missouri River, you'd be lucky to do five miles a day, and you're talking about thousands of miles upstream. These days it would be considered impossible.'

We offer Matthew a place to rest his head in our spacious tent, but he insists that he would prefer to sleep as usual, under the stars, a machete, a Bible and a transistor radio by his side.

We awake at dawn and brew up a coffee. It's show day, after all. We bid Matthew farewell and wish him the very best on his epic, seemingly impossible, Huckleberry Finn-like journey south, down the Big Muddy to the Gulf of Mexico.

'This has been the experience of a lifetime. This will go down as one of the biggest adventures of my life!' are his final thoughts for us as he bids us farewell, waving his hat in one hand as he paddles with the other, away through the gentle waves.

FOUR

OPEN-AIR CONCERT, HIGH ON A CHALK BLUFF

Plus Kansas City by truck

It's time to drag our own boat back into the river and crank up the engine. After a few miles, travelling between spectacular chalk bluffs – quite a sight after two days of largely unchanging topography – we arrive at a tiny, anonymous jetty, denoting our arrival in the jurisdiction of Les Bourgeois Vineyards. We phone up to the winery and, lo and behold, our host and a friend turn up on four-wheeled motorbikes to carry the equipment and ourselves up the hill to a stage perched on top of a 200-foot bluff. In almost every direction we can see the wide Missouri.

As I practise the songs with Kliph, W. Raymond Wood, America's greatest authority on John Evans, turns up with his son. Wood is a professor of archaeology at Missouri University, just a few miles away in Columbia.

I introduce him to the new John and pester him for information.

He claims that John is his all-time hero.

I tell him, 'We're on some kind of journey of verification, and it seems the only way to fully – well, obviously we can't fully under-stand – but just travelling these distances has given us some kind of appreciation of the magnitude of Evans's journey.'

He laughs and agrees that Evans wasn't set too much of a task when two centuries ago he rowed his way upstream just below the rock we're standing on. The Spanish simply requested him to 'expel the British and go on to the Pacific and bring back some seashells so we know that you were there', Wood says.

We laugh out loud and head to the bar for a cold beer with John Evans's felt avatar.

As it's an open-air show, our concert is divided into three sets to take advantage of the natural surroundings. It starts with a mellow, largely acoustic opening, which gives time for the sun fully to disappear over the brow of the Missouri basin behind us, and is followed, once darkness is established, by the PowerPoint presentation on John Evans's journey, which seems all the more plausible in this location, somehow.

I sing a new song, which imagines Evans in his new guise as a Spanish agent.

> I am the last conquistador,
> I am well-meaning and my intentions are earnest.
> I am the first to document,
> My route is new and my spirit enlightened.
>
> I kept hold of your letters,
> But maybe it would be better if they burn.
> Still I'm the last conquistador,
> I keep on going, though the going ain't easy.
>
> And now my mind's in farrago,
> All jumbled up, in the promise of empire.
> I'm still searching for Beula,
> And one day I will hold her in my arms.

The finale is amped-up and fuzzy – Kliph's Bonham-like beats crashing and echoing between the cliffs above the moonlit Missouri, which glows as it winds its way into the distance. It's a Friday night and an excited contingent have descended on this rural idyll from Columbia, to sit on picnic benches that cover, along with a border of fragrant pine trees, a natural slope that leads down to the stage. A large indigenous tree behind us stops us from bundling over the side of this high ledge into the river below. The moon is so big that I imagine a large holographic wolf howling in front of it.

I channel this lurid image into the howliest song in my repertoire, 'In a House with No Mirrors (You'll Never Get Old)' – a case of delusional thinking, obviously, though I imagine that, in general, delusion is what brings all performing artists to the stage; rational, secure, responsible and measured people don't feel the need. Security has never been widely available for the touring musician, and although most will attempt well-meaning experiments in social responsibility during long careers (charity concerts, etc.), musicians (speaking for myself) are in general highly irresponsible people.

With the audience in high spirits, Avatar John is mobbed after the show and everyone has their photo taken with him on their techno-phones, in smiling groups, one after another, pictures that they instantly beam up to a distant cloud. This John photo frenzy is an ideal situation as it gives Kliph and me an opportunity to pack up the equipment under the night stars. In fact, by the time we've finished, the bar has already shut, diminishing the opportunities that one would imagine arise from playing at a vineyard.

While the Columbia bourgeoisie head for home, we sit with new friends on a bench and, too tired for conversation, watch Democracy Now! videos on the palmtop, scanning the horizon occasionally as we wait for that holographic wolf to appear in the sky, where once Evans walked below, responsibly delusional, through the Midwestern wilderness.

THE TRUCK TO KANSAS CITY

It's a new dawn on the Missouri. We leave our boat at the vineyard and hitchhike into town, where our bus, our home, is waiting for us, driven here carefully from St Louis by Kliph's friend Doug, a member of the band Major Games, who seems to wear a stripy long-sleeved T-shirt at all times and never takes off his sunglasses, giving him a sophisticated aura of a screen-printing technician cum film-maker at Warhol's factory. We head west towards Kansas City, where Kliph was born. His home in Lawrence, Kansas, is just a few miles away. Located almost at the exact geographical centre-point of the USA, this is the idyllic college town where Missouri-born William Burroughs spent the last years of his life, scorning the pleasures of Tangiers and Mexico City in favour of a rural, shamanic existence in the American interior. We drop off the still-sunglassed Doug (even though it's now night-time) at a Kansas City truck-stop, where he's arranged a pickup. Then we buy some snacks for the road and continue with our endeavour on the trail of John (Don Juan) (Jean) Evans.

FIVE

NORTHWARD BOUND

In which John Evans finally reaches
the first tribes of the Missouri basin

Having followed the Missouri from its mouth in St Louis, we have been travelling steadily westwards for around 300 miles. Now at Kansas City the river begins to turn and we have to head north to follow its banks upstream.

Around 150 miles upriver from today's Kansas City the Mackay–Evans expedition first encountered the Oto tribe. It was 14 October and they were one league south of the mouth of the Platte River, just south of today's Omaha City, Nebraska. As they turned their orientation northwards, the seasons were changing and the mean teeth of winter starting to appear.

A meeting was arranged through an interpreter, whereupon General Mackay threatened the chief with a show of strength before presenting him with gifts to try to secure a right of passage upriver, a typically colonial procedure that was also used repeatedly by Lewis and Clark, according to their journals. Evans's own journals, true to his ghost-like historical status, are for the most part lost, but tantalizing fragments remain, and we can fill in the gaps regarding this journey by reading the more complete journals of the commandant, General Mackay:

October 14, 1795

On this day I reached a place one league below the mouth of the Chato
[Platte] *River. I camped in that place in order to visit the Othochita*
[Otos] *and take fresh provisions there. On the following day I reached*
a place one-half league above the said river, in order to construct a
house for the wintering of the traders whom I left there on the 20th day
... The principal men of said tribe arrived to the number of sixty. On
the following day I assembled the chiefs in council.

The Otos' previous experience of British and Spanish traders was
pretty bad, Mackay continues, 'In respect to the fact that they had
never, until the present, had any but traders who deceived them by
telling them all sorts of lies, in order to get hold of their furs, only
giving them great promises which never were fulfilled.' So he goes
in with the hard sell:

I told them that their Father [the king of Spain] *in his desire to render*
them happy, had formed a company to supply them with all the things
that they needed; that this Company, of which I am here as its agent,
would never deceive them in its promises, if they behaved well toward us.

He deems it a successful meeting:

After this speech ... I perceived that it had not failed to produce an
effect, because, although they were accustomed to pillaging the boats
destined for the most distant posts, they absolutely did not touch a
thing, except what I wished to present to them of my own accord, and
they did not even dare to enter into any of the pirogues laden with goods
for the Mandans and other tribes of the Upper Missouri.

The journey along the Otos' section of the Missouri River had indeed been a great success: 'I remained eleven days with the Othoctatas in order to make them some suggestions and attract them by means of mildness to our side.' Here, according to A. P. Nasatir in *Before Lewis and Clark: Documents Illustrating the History of the Missouri, 1785–1804* (1952), Mackay delegated the destruction of a rival British fort, or blockhouse, on the Platte River to John Evans himself. He dutifully followed the order by bombarding the abandoned wooden fort using light artillery, in all probability a small cannon. If this is the case, then Evans must have been an exceedingly good pyromaniac, as according to W. Raymond Wood there is no evidence that this blockhouse was ever built and there are certainly no known archaeological remains.

The expeditionary force continued their journey north, but a far greater test was to follow, as Mackay continues in his journal:

On November 3, the son of Pájaro Negro [Blackbird], who was in St Louis the past summer, came to meet me with a band of young men, as soon as he heard of my speedy arrival among his tribe . . . They accompanied me overland for the two days' march to their village. The cold and the snow have been so great that my voyage has been retarded considerably.

The Mackay–Evans expedition had reached the Omaha tribe, and Chief Blackbird took orders from nobody.

SIX

THE IMPASSIONED HEART

OF

OMAHA, NEBRASKA, 'THE MOST INEBRIATED STATE IN THE AMERICAS'

*Including Kliph and Griph's visit to Arc Studios
and a most memorable concert at the Slowdown*

When Splott-born Mark Bowen's Wichita record label signed Conor Oberst's young collective Bright Eyes for the European continent at the turn of the third millennium, did he realize that twenty-year-old Conor was about to become the impassioned moral heart of his generation? I think he did. Through a series of emotional and political records released on the fledgling local Saddle Creek label and produced by Oberst's friend Mike Mogis over the next decade, under the guise of Bright Eyes (poetic confessionals on the impossibility, beauty and anguish of existence), Desaparecidos (punk-rock political musings and activism relating to the American suburban experience and its place in the wider world) and Conor Oberst and the Mystic Valley Band (a liberated excursion into good-time Americana, mysticism and friendship), Oberst has followed a unique musical path and engaged directly with the American condition more eloquently than any other performer.

In that first decade of the new millennium, Conor, Mike, the Saddle Creek record label and a myriad of bands, including The Faint, Cursive and neo-tap-dancers Tilly and the Wall, have helped to redefine the face of Omaha, often noted for being the birthplace to some of the more divisive aspects of American culture, such as the Enola Gay bomber, the Swanson & Sons' TV dinner, the Enron corporation and business magnate Warren Buffett.

All this, only twenty miles north and within a couple of centuries of Mackay and Evans's meeting with the Otos at the Platte River. Back then, the site of downtown Omaha was open grassland, part of a cross-continental ecosystem comparable to the Amazon rainforest in scale and richness, which also acted as a highly sustainable and fertile hunting and foraging ground for the Omaha nation. Within a century and a half, a civilization capable of bearing talents as diverse as Malcolm X, Marlon Brando and Ed Ruscha had developed here. The speed and extremity of the change seem breathtaking.

Into the new city we drive, this early morning, Kliph, John and I, united in the feeling that we must document the music that we've been playing at these shows. We head west to Arc Studios to cut a record.

Arc was founded in the years following Bright Eyes' international breakout album, *I'm Wide Awake It's Morning*. It's a warm, largely acoustic album, which was released the same day as an electronic companion album, *Digital Ash in a Digital Urn*. Its success allowed producer and guitarist Mike Mogis to build a complex of state-of-the-art studios within the shell of a 1980s school building, cementing his and Conor's journey from recording cassettes on a four-track to being able to record to any standard imaginable. I had previously visited the half-built studios during an inebriated night after a 2006 open-air concert in Omaha, during which I opened for Bright Eyes' homecoming show (following a transcontinental tour of Canada, when we played memorably to a nest of eagles in a Vancouver park). The concert culminated in dramatic fashion when Conor Oberst launched into a fiery speech slamming the mayor of Omaha – who was present – for his regressive educational policies, as overhead a violent storm thundered over and rained on a cheering crowd that measured 15,000-strong.

Today, the songs flow out like keen whiskey from a tap. Mogis's production skills capture the colossal volume of Kliph's drums, John relaxes by the piano as I try to hit those high notes, and, one after another, songs inspired by John Evans's journey flood out, hot, to tape. 'American Interior', 'Walk into the Wilderness', 'Lost Tribes', '100 Unread Messages', 'Year of the Dog', 'Y Gwenan Gorn', 'Sugar Inside the Gun', 'Iolo', 'The Swamp', 'Last Conquistador' and 'The Whether (or Not)', all recorded, rough and ready, within a few hours, powered by nine mugs of hot coffee and an occasional dip into one of the fruit hampers bought as gifts for the elders of the UMO^nHO^n tribe, whom we hope to meet with tomorrow.

Elated, we cart the drums back to the truck and head down to a street that is the physical manifestation of what a strong musical community can create together: tonight we are to play at the Slow-down, a club opened by the Saddle Creek crew to ensnare touring bands who used to ignore Omaha on national tours, and to provide a stage for budding Omaha musicians. Built with the proceeds and reputation of the fine, uncompromising records they've released, they've attracted a number of other like-minded people to open up on the strip, which is also home to the label, here on North 14th Street, a formerly dilapidated part of town.

I kick off with the latest instalment of my song '100 Unread Messages':

Defected to the Spanish,
You joined a mighty crown,
Up the Missouri,
Flags were coming down.

You traded with the Omaha,
The Ponca and the Sioux,
But missed the Padoucas
After all the ballyhoo.

The show is wild! McCarthy Trenching opens up with his observational songwriting, which brings to mind the stories of Raymond Carver, and eventually joins Kliph, Conor, John and me in a super-weird, drunk rendition of Kevin Ayers's 'Singing a Song in the Morning' after an aborted take on the song 'Whale Trail', which falls into a cacophony of computer-game noises after we invite an audience member to play along.

Relaxing with the band after the show, we are thoroughly enjoying our Nebraska experience and conversation turns to its population. Conor is in his element, in full Desaparecidos mode:

Nebraska is what it is. I've gone back and forth between sticking up for this place with all my heart and just dissing it, like this is the most horrible place . . . But there's some good people here. I was actually proud of the crowd here even though it was a small crowd . . . I felt like their attention span was good and I was . . . I was stoked with the fact that they stuck with it from beginning to end. I think the more you can get as far as the story of America as a whole the more you can get to the truth of the story that's the important thing, because we're obviously inundated with all these false stories from our schoolbooks and from our history books . . . we're not really taught the real history. And I think that that was your point . . . we're all still trying to figure out our own history and the story of the indigenous people of America is one of the most untold stories ever. A lot of people were erased from the earth when the Europeans came to this continent. And no one wants to talk about that, no one wants to deal with that . . . if we're ever going to get right with ourselves and get right with our history we have to . . . This country it has a lot of beautiful attributes but it was founded on two of the biggest sins that were ever committed by humankind: the genocide of Native Americans and the slavery of the African Americans. And that's why we became a powerful nation. I think we all want to get at . . . the truth. Which is something that's completely ignored by public education or conventional education in America . . . they don't deal with the Native American period. I mean to me . . . the genocide of the Native Americans is one of the saddest things that's ever happened upon this earth.

THE OMAHA NATION

Omaha, or UMO^{n}HO^n, translates as 'Against the Current' and is a suitable name for a people who, in the seventeenth century, migrated to present-day Nebraska up the Mississippi and Missouri rivers from an area at the confluence of the Ohio and Wabash rivers. The explorer Jacques Marquette first placed them on the map in 1673 when he noted their village at Bow Creek. Along with the Kansa, Quapaw, Osage and Ponca, the Omaha is one of the five Dhegiha tribes that form part of the Siouan family.

By 1775 the Omaha's leader, Chief Blackbird, had consolidated power in this region of the Missouri by forging trade links and hard bargains with Europeans, and his tribe, semi-nomadic equestrians, numbered over a thousand. They hunted buffalo on the Nebraska and Iowa plains, wintering in earth lodges at Big Village, near today's Macy, just downriver from Sioux City. When John Evans spent the winter of 1795/6 with the Omaha, they were at the height of their civilization.

By 1800 a smallpox epidemic had wiped out over a third of the population, including Blackbird himself, and within the next five years the tribe had halved again after another epidemic. Over the next two centuries many further hardships were to follow, including the loss of their hunting grounds and the shrinking of their lands by 75 per cent, following the formation of the Omaha Reservation in 1854.

Today, there are over 4,000 tribal members living on the reservation and a further 2,200 registered members living further afield. Unemployment has fallen by 20 per cent since the reopening in 2013 of the Blackbird Bend Casino but is still at 60 per cent, whilst youth unemployment stands at 73 per cent. Life expectancy currently stands at fifty-four.

Compared to the national American average life expectancy (according to the 2013 OECD statistics) of 78.7, this figure confirms clearly the persisting inequalities that remain between most of the inhabitants of the United States and their reservation-dwelling First Nation counterparts.

SEVEN

THE BATTLES

OF

DENNIS HASTINGS

A kind elder warrior leads us to the site of Fort Carlos

I first speak to Dennis on a payphone in a drab-looking rest area on Interstate 70, just outside Kansas City. I'd been on his website, as I was looking for a way of meeting up with the UMOⁿHOⁿ tribe and he seemed to be its leading historian, but I was ignorant of his significance to American history. We're talking away about John Evans (who's perched on top of the booth), and Dennis seems to know where the site of Fort Carlos is, which is super-exciting as I'm finally meeting someone who knows where Evans lived, and then the word 'Alcatraz' hits me out of the stream of the conversation.

'Have you heard of Alcatraz?' Dennis asks me.

'Yes,' I reply.

'I was there,' says Dennis.

'Oh!' I reply.

My mind wanders . . . what did Dennis do to deserve that most infamous of addresses?

The next day we drive on to the Omaha Reservation to pick Dennis up. I'm eager to meet him as he seems such a cool guy, but now I find myself just staring at what I perceive to be home-made prison tattoos on his hands. Shit, he really was there, I think to myself. But why?

It soon transpires that Dennis Hastings PhD was the first graduate of the New School of California to have been raised on the Omaha Reservation. He's also an anthropologist, historian, author and political activist. Despite trying to run away on countless occasions from the Native American boarding school/prison camp assimilation system, where all Native American kids used to be sent in order to become less Indian (he was sent to freezing North Dakota), he was too bright to miss his calling, and after trying out Vietnam with the Marines (which wasn't that much better than the school system), off west he went, to what at the time was arguably the global centre of counterculture, political activism and cosmology. He was never jailed there, of course, and being an ignorant tourist I had completely misunderstood the significance of Alcatraz in recent Native American history.

From 20 November 1969 until June 1971, when they were forced out after broken promises of negotiation by the authorities, Dennis was part of the occupation of Alcatraz island by activists allied with the American Indian Movement (AIM). Their objective of raising awareness of Native American land disputes with the US government and of broken treaties and impoverished living conditions (the life expectancy of tribal members in 1969 was forty-four) was achieved, however, and rekindled the flame of activism throughout the 554 tribal nations within the USA.

Dennis also took part in the 1973 occupation of Wounded Knee (site of the 1890 massacre of 300 men, women and children), when the FBI surrounded the town on the Pine Ridge Reservation with military personnel and armed vehicles during a three-month stand-off between the American State and the Oglala Lakota, who had allied themselves with AIM activists. Here the FBI faced a formidable opponent: almost all the Native American young men had been given full military training in the Marines and were no pushovers. The affair was prolonged further by divisions within the reservation that had turned it into what was at the time the murder capital of the US. Activist Leonard Peltier remains in jail to this day, having been convicted, with scant evidence, of the murder of an FBI officer, after a shoot-out at Pine Ridge in 1975.

The story of John Evans interests Dennis, because even though Evans was working for a colonial power, his tale reveals a piece of history that lies outside the official accounts of the US. Avatar John sits in the front of the truck and guides us a few miles down a valley and over a ridge on to a plain of cornfields near the Nebraska–Iowa border. Archaeologists have only been able to speculate as to the location of the original Omaha village and the Fort Carlos trading post, but here we are being taken there.

'This is where the Missouri used to flow. It changes course every so often,' says Dennis.

It's 90 degrees, but we get out of the truck regardless and walk a pathway through the middle of a cornfield.

'That's Iowa over there,' he says.

We gaze across the corn flats towards some huge power plants in the distance, which are billowing out vast clouds of smoke into the blue skies.

'Behind us here are the old bluffs. The village and the fort would have been just around here.'

Lacking the expert eye of an archaeologist, and walled in by six-foot corn plants, I'm finding it pretty difficult to visualize anything, but after a while I begin to picture the fort up towards the bluff – a fantastic spot – and just below it, on the old shoreline, the site of the

Omaha 'Big Village', in those days possibly a bigger settlement than many of the American villages that Evans had passed through.

As General Mackay described in his journals, 'The location of the fort seems to have been prepared by nature. It is in a commanding district, which rises for a circumference of about one thousand feet. It looks on the shore to the river, as if to command the rest of the area.'

There Evans would have heard the Omaha songs and eaten their food. We know he was a flute (probably what we know as a whistle) player, so it's likely he would have played and sung them his favourite Welsh songs and hymns. Dennis is intrigued by this thought and by the fact that our cultures were exposed to one another over 200 years ago. He asks me to sing some songs for him, so we go to the back of the truck and I try a few of my own numbers.

He is not impressed by my Anglo-American stylings (even though sung in Welsh). 'Play me the real stuff, the songs John Evans would have sung,' he says.

I dig out the photocopy of 'Rywbeth Arall i'w Wneuthur', written by Evans's friend Dafydd Ddu Eryri, which fellow Evans enthusiast Menna Jones had given me in Waunfawr.

'Rywbeth arall i'w . . .' I sing out, a cappella.

Dennis appears more relaxed now. We put a Pigyn Clust CD on the stereo, as they know how to sing these songs properly, then drive back into the reservation to visit the village of Rosalie, where artist Margery Coffee and her family have set up a community group to reclaim the disused banks in the village, which were originally built in order to sell off tribal lands to European settlers.

'This is a very typical prairie town,' Margery tells us. 'You look at the buildings down there and they all look alike. Well, the fronts were made by Sears – you could order them through its catalogue, they would arrive and then you built a box, a brick building, behind them.'

She's been joined by her son's family in the reconstruction of this dilapidated prairie village high street, which they hope to transform into a progressive solar-powered community, with a farmers' market, shops and artists' studio, here in this 'far-flung corner of the world', as she puts it.

'Yes, the time is now,' she declares. 'Self-sustaining is where it's at. These huge corporations are dinosaurs; they're going to die of their own size. And we are going to have to learn to get along with each other and to work together as a community in order to survive.' This echoes Matthew Batten's sentiments on the river just a few days ago. She's also horrified with America's 'Hollywoodized' self-image and with the corporate takeover of the government and the military.

'America's in deep danger of falling apart, just like the Russians did,' she continues, 'because they cannot sustain this idiocy. And what does a poor little tribe do who's been beholden to this mega-government? We're going to try to teach them to go back to the land and survive. I don't know with global warming how long that's going to be, because the prognosis for that is horrible. This whole area is supposed to be unlivable by 2050.'

We drive back pensively through Macy, the UMO^{n}HO^{n}s' capital, where it's noticeable how few cars there are: there isn't one parked outside each home, as is the case in suburban America. The supposed top-down paradigm of American wealth distribution just doesn't seem to trickle down here to the reservation. Dennis, however, remains positive and keeps looking to the future. He is currently involved in a project to build a museum of Omaha culture so that all the kids who grow up on the reservation can feel a sense of belong-ing, which wasn't the case during his upbringing in the days of

assimilation. Nebraska-born architect Vincent Graves, a former asso-
ciate of Frank Gehry, has proposed constructing an ambitious
building atop a sacred bluff overlooking the Missouri River. The
exhibits will include objects such as their Sacred Pole, a cherished
wooden stick that represents the Venerable Man, also known as 'the
Original Omaha', and the ceremonial White Buffalo Robe, both of
which are now repatriated from the Smithsonian and Harvard Mu-
seums, thanks to Dennis's diplomatic work. All I can think about is
that Evans would have experienced the sacred powers of these relics
in the days of the mighty Blackbird.

EIGHT

UNICORNS
OF THE
WILD FRONTIER

*Evans's search for the wonders of the
American interior and the Pacific Ocean*

*There is, they say, on the long chain of Rockies which you will cross to go to
the Pacific Ocean, an animal which has only one horn on its forehead. Be very
particular in the description which you will make of it if you will be unable to
procure one of this kind.*

This instruction, one of many given to John Evans by his superior
General Mackay, illustrates better than anything the unknown
quantity that was the American West. Europeans simply didn't know
what was out there, and contemporary maps could only speculate
as to what lay in the interior. The first Surveyor General of Upper
Louisiana was Antoine Soulard and his 1795 map depicted the source
of the Missouri River as being way out west in what we would now
consider Oregon, rather than its true location in the northern state
of Montana. The vast Rocky Mountains were thought to be a one-
mountain-wide range that could be hopped over in a day or two
before a short walk to the Pacific Ocean and a 2,000-peso reward
from the governor of Spanish Louisiana.

James Mackay's instructions to John Evans are dated 28 January 1796, at which time the Missouri River, according to this Spanish Scott, was 'completely frozen'. From Evans's 1797 letter to Samuel Jones we can gather that, in the meantime, he had been on a 25-day bison hunt with members of the Omaha tribe, beginning on 21 November, when the food supplies at both the Omaha Big Village and Fort Carlos were completely finished. Some believe the supposed bison hunt to be one of Evans's more fanciful inventions, based on stories of Mackay's hunts in central Nebraska a few months later. Yet the known documents in the Spanish archives do nothing to disprove Evans's claim, and one doubts that there was any reason for John Evans, in this case, to exaggerate what was already an extreme experience.

In early February, Evans was once again dispatched as the leader of what was at least a three-man group, along with the French-speaking boatmen Scarlet and Tollibois, who were both respected by Mackay for their conduct and perseverance, this time with the aim of reaching the Mandan tribe and, in time, the Pacific. On 19 February, Mackay writes in the tone of a beloved close friend to John Evans: 'Mr Evans, I have found the time tedious since you left . . . however, I begin to get accustomed to live sollitary I dare say that in the course of some time hence I shall be happy alone as the Indian in the Desert.' But Evans was back soon enough, his mission aborted when he disturbed a Lakota hunting party, which chased him for four leagues and forced him and his lieutenants to retreat almost 300 miles back to Fort Carlos.

As Mackay writes in his journal:

Mr Evans ascended the Missouri as high as the White River about 80 leagues* above the Mahas, their having been met by a Nation called Sious of the Grand Detour, who generally pass the Spring and Autumn on the borders of the White River, was obliged to return to the Maha Post. Those Indians having discovered Mr Evans near their Camp they persued him near 4 leagues descending the River and would have probably stopt him, if the Weather and the Aproach of the night had not favoured his retreat.

With the Lakota (Sioux) tribes to the north wreaking havoc on the Spanish expedition's hope of reaching the Mandans before the following winter, Mackay sent another messenger to seek out the Lakota. A conference was arranged within a month of Evans's return, with

---

* A league on dry land is roughly the distance walked within one hour, or in most official instances (but not all) three miles.

four principal Lakota chiefs, Blackbird of the Omaha and General Mackay.

Mackay, however, was reluctant to leave Chief Blackbird's side. He now referred to him as a 'Prince' and pleaded in letters with his superiors at the Missouri Company in St Louis and with Spanish Louisiana's government in New Orleans to furnish him with further gifts to appease the fearsome chief's insatiable demands.

'[Do] not doubt that my friend the Maha Prince [Blackbird] has the right to a generous recompense,' writes Mackay in his Missouri Company journal, continuing:

[I]*t is important to sustain the authority of this intrepid man by the ostentation and particular distinction of elevating him above any other chief . . . it is better to fatten one who rules as a despot over various tribes, than feed many at less expense . . . the Government must come to our aid, for he is one of the chief supporters of our navigation. The intrigue of the English, in order to attract the tribes of the Missouri, has planted deep roots among these peoples, that it is necessary to apply a prompt remedy, unless we desire to see ourselves exposed to abandon this magnificent country which must some day be a great resource to the prosperity and the glory of the state.*

Mackay had identified Chief Blackbird as his main ally in breaking the tribal embargo on the Missouri River and rebuffing the influence and threat of the English traders from Canadian lands to the north (who had already unfurled a Union Jack at a trading post in Mandan lands). With Mackay therefore busy establishing his presence with the Omaha, he once again decided to send Evans and his small party upriver, this time with the blessing of at least some of the many Lakota tribes.

Mackay, pondering on the man he had again chosen to lead the Spanish from the Omaha nation into unchartered lands and retake the Mandan trading post in the name of the Spanish king, mused: 'I sent an expedition from the Maha Post under the command of Mr John T. Evans a young man of Upright Character on whose Perseverance and ability I could entirely rely.' Evans's quest to reach the Mandan tribe and the promised land of the lost tribe of the Madogwys was back on. He was also once again master of his own destiny, albeit funded by the Spanish king, for whom Evans was now, as Gwyn Williams pointed out, the 'last conquistador' in the whole of the Americas.

CONCERT AT UMOⁿHOⁿ NATION HIGH-SCHOOL GYMNASIUM

NO CHEESE PRODUCTS IN THE GYMNASIUM, reads a large sign as we load our equipment into the high-school gym.

This concert was always touch and go: the sprinkler system at the school had been damaged and the concert was called off, but it's fixed now and the school has reopened.* We have, as instructed, brought five hampers of fruit that will be distributed amongst the tribal elders, and before we do anything, Granma, the UMOⁿHOⁿ nation's elder and leading practitioner of their language, must deliver a sermon. Everyone lowers their heads in respect.

Then we sit on the bottom bench of the bleachers as the four members of the nation's White Tail Singers prepare to perform.

---

* The school has Native Studies on the curriculum, and although hardly ideal, when everything could plausibly be taught through the medium of UMOⁿHOⁿ, there's a huge difference in attitude since the education policies of assimilation. At least the kids are taught about where they come from, which is also the drive behind the plans for the museum.

'You know the average age on the reservation today?' Dennis asks after Granma finishes.

'I dunno, forty-six?' I gamble.

'It's nineteen and a half,' says Dennis, proudly smiling at the increasing population and young outlook of this tiny nation.

A lot of young people are in the audience (it's a ticket out of class), mixed in with elders, teachers and a few curious members of the community.

The four members of the White Tail Singers sit in a circle, wearing sportswear, and finish eating their pizza (in contravention of the ban on cheese products). They then get to singing. They bang a large shared floor-bound drum in unison and chant beautiful UMO^{n}HO^n-language songs, some traditional, some more recent. It's extremely loud – it doesn't require a PA system and would stun an audience anywhere in the world. 'How do you follow that?' we wonder.

The plan is for us and the White Tail Singers to play songs one after another, like a tag team, so it's our turn now. Kliph has his drums set up, and we play a series of Welsh-language songs. It seems to be going OK: at least, people clap along and don't leave, always a good sign. And once we finish a song, we know the White Tail Singers will follow with an amazing energetic banger. Then it's time for my PowerPoint presentation on John Evans's life and journey.

Richard, Margery's husband from the village of Rosalie, comes up after the show. Having gone to a lot of trouble to organize the event, he feels my performance was a little too loose and that I look like I need a decent night's sleep.

Dennis comes to my defence: 'This is what happened 200 years ago,' he says, with a large smile. 'It's a historically significant occasion: our cultures have met up again and we're all still here!'

He pats John on the back and we give Dennis, who's by now our new hero, a ride home in the truck.

We wish him many farewells, then drop Kliph and his drums at a car park, where that legend of the road, Joe Puleo, whom we haven't seen for weeks now, has come to the rescue, picking up Kliph in a brown Honda five-seater saloon. Kliph will proceed no further with John and me on our northern endeavour, and heads south for a Flaming Lips rehearsal in Oklahoma City. We now realize that his journey with the Avatar John, from St Louis to the UMO^{n}HO^n nation, has geographically mirrored Mackay's own journey with the flesh-and-blood Evans. I wonder if Kliph has Scottish blood?

NINE

THE LONGITUDE AND LATITUDE OF CHIEF JEAN EVANS (FRANCOPHILE RIVER-MAN AND SPANISH CHIEF OF THE ROCKY MOUNTAINS)

*And his cartographic journey to
(and sojourn at) the lands of the Arikara*

On 8 June 1796, Evans writes in his journal:

*After having received from Mr James McKay [sic], Agent of the
Missouri Company the necessary instructions, as well as men, Provisions and Merchandizes, I set off from the Missouri Company's
establishment at the Maha village, to ascend the Missouri as far as the
Pacific Ocean . . .*

According to the correspondence of Trudeau, the French-speaking
governor of St Louis and partner in the Missouri Company, Mackay
had sent three men to advance towards the Pacific. John Evans as the
leader was expected to follow his commandant's instructions to the

letter. And at long last Evans's brief period as a surveyor in Baltimore and his more recent time in the company of the experienced navigator Mackay were to come to the fore. A seven-part series of maps in the possession of the Beinecke Library at Yale University is testament to Evans's skills as a cartographer, and duly provides us with a detailed account of his journey towards the Madogwys.

Although Evans had abandoned his previous attempt to reach the Pacific following the Lakota's attack, the subsequent peace treaty negotiated between Mackay, Blackbird and the four Lakota tribal leaders would have allowed Evans to journey by river rather than by land, as specified clearly by Mackay's instructions. According to W. Raymond Wood, this is certainly what happened, as the great detail in which the river is depicted in the Beinecke Library maps proves.

The seven panels of these maps were thought for over a century to be the work of the explorer William Clark of Lewis and Clark fame, but although they are drawn in Clark's hand, they are copies of Evans's original. In 1946 Aubrey Diller recognized by date deduction alone that the true author could only have been John Evans. In fact, Evans's map had been sent to Meriwether Lewis on 13 January 1804 by President Jefferson himself, with the note, 'I now enclose you a map of the Missouri . . . It is said to be very accurate, having been done by a Mr Evans by order of the Spanish Government.'

Travelling with men who were presumably experienced, French-speaking *voyageurs*, Evans made sure to follow Mackay's instructions to note the distance, latitude and longitude of his route. And in doing so he mapped and even came up with his own names for some of the rivers and creeks he passed. Indeed, Bernard DeVoto confirms in his book *The Course of Empire* (1952) that the first known written reference to the Yellowstone River is in Mackay's letter to Evans, and Evans would become the first to place it on a map. W. Raymond Wood agrees that Evans's map provides the earliest place names for this area of the Missouri basin. Most of these place names have continued in use to the present time, although some have been translated to English.' He judges that Evans used a compass and sextant, together with a chronometer, to compose his map, and informs us that if you overlay it on modern maps, there is 'little deviation from reality', which is highly surprising, given the difficulty of Evans's circumstances. Wood explains the procedure further in his book *Prologue to Lewis and Clark*:

> Determining latitude was a relatively simple matter. A sextant, usually made of brass, was used to observe the altitude of the sun or a star above the horizon. Latitude was then ascertained using the resulting readings together with a book of astronomical tables. Determining longitude, however, was another matter entirely. Evans would have to know the precise Greenwich time at the sun's Meridian passage at the position he was attempting to determine.

Luckily, Avatar John and I have a GPS installed in our truck.

THE LAND OF THE LAKOTA

The 'Sioux', an offensive catch-all term coined by their enemies the Ojibwe and mispronounced by the French, who used it to refer to numerous nations belonging to the same linguistic group – the Lakota, Dakota and Nakota and their multitude of descendant tribes – were the dominant warring presence in this area of the river and way beyond, for hundreds of miles to the east and west. Pushed out of their lands in Minnesota by European pioneers, the Lakota dominated the plains and frustrated the relative tranquillity of their other linguistic relatives, the Mandan and the Omaha, to the north and south respectively.

A few fragments aside, any detailed topographical journals which Evans presumably kept are lost, but along with the ghostly traces of his maps, entries in the journals of Lewis and Clark, who undertook the same journey eight years later, help to depict the scene. Lewis, who also boasted some Welsh ancestry, states on Monday 17 September 1804 that he observed in one day in the region of the Corvus creek:

[B]*arking squiril* [prairie dogs] . . . *a great number of wolves of the small kind, halks* [hawks] *and some pole cats were to be seen* [. . .] *to the West a high range of hills, strech across the country from N. to S. and appeared distant about 20 miles* [. . .] *this senery already rich pleasing and beatiful was still farther hightened by immence herds of Buffaloe, deer Elk and Antelopes which we saw in every direction feeding on the hills and plains. I do not think I exagerate when I estimate the number of Buffaloe which could be compre*[hend]*ed at one view to amount to 3000.*

We can only imagine the wonder and the worries that Evans experienced in this very same pristine wilderness. To put behind him the harsh winter months, the aborted missions, illness, internment, and finally to make steady meaningful progress towards his cherished goal, must have been insanely exciting.

As Evans passed, and documented, the White and Bad rivers that flow from the famed Badlands to the west into the great muddy Missouri, he may have come across a camp of the Teton branch of the Lakota. He would certainly have been carrying gifts for the Arikara and Mandan tribes, as well as some limited supplies for his trek to the Pacific. So it's not impossible that the Spanish flags mentioned in a brief description by William Clark in a 26 September 1804 entry in his journal were gifts from Evans's hands. Would he have had a similar experience to Clark's at the hands of the Tetons?

[A]*bout 10 Well Dressd. young Men who took me up in a roabe highly adecrated and Set me Down by the Side of their Chief on a Dressed Robe in a large Council House, this house formed a ¾ circle of Skins Well Dressed and Down together under this Shelter about 70 Men Set forming a Circle in front of the Cheifs a plac of 6 feet Diameter was Clear and the pipe of peace raised on Sticks under wich there was swans down scattered, on each Side of this Circle two Pipes, the (two) flags of Spain & the flag we gave them in front of the Grand Chief a large fire was near in which provisions were Cooking, in the Center about 400 lbs. of excellent Buffalo Beef as a present for us.*

A few miles upstream there is firm proof that Lewis and Clark were indeed following Evans's map, as Clark eventually tried to erase Evans's mistaken marking of a volcano on the west bank of the Missouri in what is now Gregory County, South Dakota. An amalgamated copy of Evans's map in Mackay's hand, currently available to view at the Library of Congress in Washington, DC, and known as the Indian Office Map, also reveals this supposed volcano. It's perhaps unsurprising that Evans, a Welshman in a strange land, failed to recognize what must have been only an open sore of burning coal in the Earth's surface. There was nothing there to be seen eight years later, however, as Clark points out on 18 October 1804:

I walked on shore in the evening with a view to See some of those remarkable places mentioned by evins, none of which I could find. The country in this quarter is generally leavel & fine some short hills, and some ragid rangers of Hills at a distance.

It seems he was right to try to scratch out the volcano on his Evans-derived map, but what this passage by Clark does suggest is that he was in possession of a written description by Evans of this area. If that is the case, it gives credence to the belief that many more of Evans's journal entries once existed and that they are indeed unfortunately lost.*

Still the rivers and creeks and mounds and bluffs kept coming. The first European explorer to reach these parts had been Étienne de Veniard, sieur de Bourgmont, in 1714, followed by Pierre Gaultier de Varennes, sieur de La Vérendrye in 1738 and his son, Pierre, Chevalier de La Vérendrye, five years later. A succession of French-speaking itinerant boatmen and traders followed them, so, for the most part, place names were translations of pre-existing Native American names translated by French-speaking interpreters. Evans was also keeping an eye out for Jean Baptiste Truteau, the Missouri Company trader who was hoped to be still alive somewhere along the river, stranded following the previous, failed Missouri Company expedition that had departed St Louis two years earlier. Ominously, though, Evans had already passed Truteau's deserted wooden fort, Ponca House.

Cape Clear, R. au Kenvill, Petite Arch, Rapid That Wonders, Solitary Island, Half Mast Island, 3 Sisters Island, Big Bend, Good Humor Island, Sentenel Shoe, Otter River, Friendship, Kakawissassa and Bomb River came and went and were documented for posterity, and after two long months John Evans finally reveals in an existing part of his journal:

---

* The surviving journal entries were discovered within Mackay's own papers.

After a long and fatiguing voyage I arrived the 8th of August following at the Village of the Rik,ka,ras on the South Side of the Missouri, 250 leagues above the Mahas, I here met with some difficulties to get along, the Rik,karas would not permit me to pass their Village and carry my Goods to those nations that reside above them, they said, they were themselves in want of Goods &c. Finding then that all my Efforts were in vain, to get on, I was obliged to stay among them.

Just as Truteau had found before him, the Arikaras were wary of letting goods upriver to the Mandans and the Hidatsas, especially if they were carrying arms of any description.

In fact, Truteau had only been allowed to leave the Arikaras in June, and he and Evans had somehow missed each other on the river as Truteau fled south, for St Louis. An entry in Truteau's journal gives us an indication of the nomadic existence of the population at the time: 'The Arikara, called for short the Ree, had their dwellings ten leagues higher upon the left bank. These they abandoned during my stay among them [due to Lakota incursions, GR], in order to withdraw nearer to the Mandan, one can count five hundred warriors of this nation' – implying a large total population of a few thousand men, women and children.

The enforced stay with the Arikaras became an opportunity for Evans as he sought to look for any traces of the Welsh language in the Upper Missouri and beyond. The Arikaras, or Sahnish as they prefer to call themselves, played host to a number of tribes from the far west during Evans's stay. Here, once more, Evans's own journal reveals some meaningful details:

Some Weeks after my arrival, several Indians of different nations particularly the Caneenawees and Shayenns habitants of the Rocky

Mountains, came to the village to see me. Their Chief in a very long and prolix discourse expressed to me the joy they felt to see the Whites, they assured me of their Love and Attachment for their Great father the Spaniard and for all the children who Came in their Country.

With his newly acquired knowledge of the tribal civilizations of the American interior, and his new-found status of travelling Spanish chief in the eyes of the nations he encountered, it was certainly an interesting time for Evans, even if he was technically under arrest. Finally, after a six-week sojourn, he saw an opportunity to talk himself out of the situation: 'Judging it necessary for the better insuring the success of my enterprise to take the possession of the fort built at the Mandaine village by the traders of Canada, I succeeded in persuading the Rikaras to let me go so far as there with some goods.' Evans had successfully broken the Arikaras' blockade. The next tribe he would come across upriver was the fabled Mandan – or, as he dearly hoped, the lost tribe of the Madogwys.

TEN

LOST TRIBES

Beer at Bismarck Sushi Bar

D riving up the eastern side of the mighty Missouri, having crossed the river from the UMO^{n}HO^n nation, we leave Nebraska and enter a corner of Iowa at Sioux City, which is on the border with South Dakota. Soon enough we are in North Dakota. The climate changes drastically as winter sets in early, just as it did for John Evans, and as we zoom the truck up through the darkness of the 83, still on the east flank of the river, just a few miles from the Standing Rock Reservation on the west side, where Sitting Bull lived and died and where the Mountain Time Zone begins, the snow and ice have become precarious and an unexpected gust blows the whole vehicle off the road; it scurries out of control through the pack snow like a giant armadillo into what is presumably, underneath the solidified tundra of the blizzard, a field (but for all we know may be a car park).

I brake the 'dillo before we reach the deepest snowdrift and, although shaken, we are reassured by kind passers-by, who stop immediately, unfazed, to help. The truck is backed up from our unfortunate destination with ease, and we continue cautiously towards Bismarck, the capital of North Dakota, in search of comfort after our near calamity.

Spotting a Japanese restaurant in a strip mall, we park up for a beer to calm our nerves. I reach instinctively to grab John from the passenger seat, but realize I'm just not in the mood. Leaving him there to guard the parked truck, I head in alone. I watch the local news channel at the restaurant bar and take note that the state legislators are relaxing gun laws, trying to close down the last abortion clinic in the whole state and opening the whole ancient land to fracking. Local basketball follows; the players seem to be shorter than the national average – maybe it's a high-school league. I love American sport, as I don't understand any of the rules, which frees me from having an impassioned opinion about something that is ultimately trivial and only complicates life (as is the case when I'm at home, supporting my local team through thick and thin – mostly thin). The people in here seem fun and friendly; there's not a gun in sight.

I return calmed, a couple of hours later, and although it's freezing cold as we settle for the night in down sleeping bags in our car-park bunk beds, the excitement about our imminent visit to the Fort Berthold Reservation, the present-day home of the Mandan, Hidatsa and Sahnish (Arikara) tribes, helps to ease away any discomfort.

We awake early, and once the sun's diffused winter beam is upon us we continue north, leaving Bismarck behind. We fill up with gas at a truck stop that sells *everything*, including souvenir North Dakota 'bird turds' (yes, they really are varnished hardened turds with wings), and head up the 83, past a series of power stations with gigantic sets of billowing chimneys that chug deep charcoal clouds at a 45-degree angle through the opaque white sky, right up to the Kármán line miles above us. In turn these power stations are served by miles of earthbound silver tubular fuel pipes with the diameter of tankers, which snake as far as the curved horizon through the otherwise featureless snow-white landscape, magnifying and reflecting the immense stratosphere in ominous monochrome.

John Evans would have travelled this way towards the Knife River Mandan settlements, charting his route carefully through the spare cottonwood and elm banks of the Missouri, clouds of a few million migrating birds flying south in the sky above, escaping the coming winter, as he dreamed of the lost tribe at night. He, like us, was almost there.

Lost tribe,
Stay free,
Lost tribe,
Deliver us from pain,
Lost tribe,
Stay free,

Lost Tribes

For you,
For me.
Lost tribes will conquer,
Lost tribes will conquer all the world,
For you,
For me,
For us,
For thee,
Lost Tribes deliver.
Lost tribes,
Deliver us from pain,
Lost tribes,
I come in peace,
For you.

ELEVEN

ARRIVAL AT THE MANDAN VILLAGES

On 23 September 1796, John Evans wrote in his journal:

I arrived at the Mandaine Village which is situated about 10 leagues above the Rikara on the Same Side (south) of the Missouri, there I was visited by the Munitarees and the Wattassoons whose villages are only a league above those of the Mandaines, those nations as well as the Mandaines received me very cordially. I gave their Chiefs in the name of the Great Father the Spaniard, who inhabits the other Side of The great lake [the king of Spain] *and in the name of the great Chief who inhabits this Side of the great Lake* [the governor of Spanish Louisiana] *and also in the name of the Chief who resides at the Entrance of the Missouri* [the governor of St Louis], *the Flags and Medals that were given me for that purpose by Mr McKay. Besides those medals & flags I made some small presents, which were received with the greatest of Satisfaction, and testified their acknowledgment in the most expressive manner . . .*

It had taken him four months to reach the Mandan villages from the Omaha. On the way he would have passed by the Mandans' abandoned former villages on the confluence of the Heart River and the Missouri, near today's state capital, Bismarck. The remains of nine large villages, such as On-a-slant, Double Ditch and Yellow Ecore, reveal a large, settled agrarian civilization acting as a transcontinental trading hub for a multitude of goods. According to W. Raymond Wood, at least 9,000 people lived in this area, although some historians estimate a people 15,000-strong. In any case, their villages were fortified and they had numbers enough not to fear any rival nomadic tribe. Smallpox arrived to devastating effect, however, in 1780 and decimated the population, leading to a forty-mile exodus to the north, where their allies, the Hidatsa people, lived in villages near the Knife River, close to its Missouri confluence.

Both the Mandans and Hidatsas were turtle-worshipping tribes of the Siouan linguistic family, who had developed and migrated centuries previously from the Ohio valley, the Mandans being the first to migrate west. According to the collective Mandan memory, when the previously nomadic Hidatsas eventually followed them to the plains, the Mandans taught them how to adapt to a settled existence. After the smallpox epidemic, the Hidatsas repaid the favour, taking the Mandans in and replenishing them with skills that had been swept away by that most terrible of diseases. Together they were better protected from their notorious rampaging cousins, the various tribes of the feared Lakota. The Hidatsa tribe helped the Mandans to rebuild their culture on the understanding that they wouldn't live upriver of the Hidatsas, an arrangement that still stands today within the Fort Berthold Reservation, which they both share with the Sahnish (Arikara), who hail from an altogether different place and belong to the Caddoan linguistic group.

By the time Evans arrived, the Mandans were based in two villages on the Knife/Missouri confluence, with two larger Hidatsa villages a few miles upstream near today's town of Stanton. In between lay a mixed village, now famous for having been the residence of Sakakawea, the female Shoshone guide to Lewis and Clark. Chief Black Cat was the main Mandan chief at the village of Ruhptare, with the younger Sheheke, or Big White, acting as chief at the smaller village of Mitutanka, near today's Deapolis, which is where Evans first landed, to much fanfare, on that September day.

The Mandans, true to their culture of hospitality, welcomed Evans, in all likelihood, with great joy and curiosity. He would have been fed an array of delicious food from their ample and hearty cuisine, and he would have felt an instantaneous relief after the hardship of travel and the uncertainty of his position at the hands of the Arikara. It appears that he spent at least five days making himself acquainted with the local villages and their chiefs.

He would also have experienced the Mandans' elaborate ceremonial culture of music, movement and decoration. Later eyewitness reports – from Lewis and Clark, the painter George Catlin, the touring Prussian ethnologist Prince Maximilian and the Swiss painter Karl Bodmer – are testament to the Mandan and Hidatsa way of life. The traditions of the Okipa ceremony and the Buffalo Dance became some of the most celebrated in Native American culture, as the tales from the prairies were relayed by book to the immigrant settlers of the new American cities. The dramatic ritual torture, whereupon young men were tested on their endurance and warrior capabilities by fasting for four days before being hung painfully by hooks to the chest from the roof of the largest earth lodge, became especially notorious. In the 1830s, George Catlin's famous paintings of the beautiful, elaborate Bull Dances and Buffalo Dances recorded these traditions for future generations, and as he wrote at the time, 'It may be thought easy to imagine such a group of naked figures, and the effect that rude painting on their bodies would have; but I am ready to declare that the most creative imagination cannot appreciate the singular beauty of these graceful figures thus decorated with various colours, reclining in groups, or set in rapid motion.'

As the autumn closed in and the winter months loomed, Evans now had a whole season to soak up the traditions and myths of his wonderful hosts. The Mandan legend of the Lone Man who had arrived up the Missouri in an ark-like canoe had fuelled speculation that he represented Prince Madog himself, and Evans would have been able to spend some time deciphering whether these great people were indeed the children of Madog.

Some romantics have speculated on whether Evans had any meaningful love affairs during his American adventures, which is certainly not implausible for a man in his mid twenties. It's likely that, for a Protestant like Evans, the sensual, spectacular and flirtatious dances he saw while staying with the Mandans would have been a curious and previously unimaginable sight. The following description of one such dance, designed to bring the warriors a great yield whilst hunting buffalo, is taken from Clark's journal, eight years after Evans's stay:

5th of January Satturday 1805

. . . a Buffalow Dance for 3 nights passed in the 1st Village, a curious custom the old men arrange themselves in a circle & after smok[ing] *a pipe which is handed by a young man, Dress*[ed] *up for the purpose, the young men who have their wives back of the Circle go* [each] *to one of the old men with a whining tone and request the old man to take his wife (who presents* [herself] *necked except a robe) and – (or Sleep with her) the girl then takes the old man (who very often can scarcely walk) and leads him to a convenient place for the business, after which they return to*

the lodge; if the old man (or a white man) returns to the lodge without
gratifying the Man & his wife, he offers her again and again; it is often
the Case that after the 2ⁿᵈ time without Kissing the Husband throws a new
robe over the old man &c and begs him not to despise him & his wife (We
sent a man to this Medisan Dance last night, they gave him 4 girls) all
this is to cause the Buffalow to Come near So that they may Kill them.

In the interest of self-preservation, the First Nations in general
encouraged marriages outside of the clan system, sometimes outside
of their respective tribes and even with explorers and traders of European ancestry. There was certainly less stigma associated with
extramarital relationships if conducted respectably within certain codes,
and indeed the writer Emyr Jones in his 1969 novella based on the life
of Evans, *Grym y Lli* ('The Force of the Current'), goes as far as to
link Evans to a Mandan woman named 'Tika'. As we may decipher
from the quote above, the Lewis and Clark expedition gained notoriety
as many of them, including perhaps Lewis himself, had contracted the
infamous European import, syphilis, on their journey and were suffering badly from the ravages of the lesions and open sores that the
condition produced during and after their lengthy expedition. Some
even attribute Lewis's suicide to the psychological effects of the disease.
Evans, however, seems to have been following General Mackay's
detailed instructions to the letter in most cases, and we have no evidence
to disprove that he also heeded the following warning from Mackay:

In your orders be strict with your detachment and take care that no offense is
committed against the nations through which you pass, especially by the
connection that they may seek to have with women, a thing which is ordinarily
the origin of dissatisfaction and discord with the savages . . .

Now, he took to another of the tasks he had been given, that of eliminating the British Canadians from operating their trade within the borders of Spanish Louisiana. And this he attempted with gusto.

THE NORTH DAKOTA OIL RUSH

'There's more oil here than in Saudi Arabia – 14,000 new jobs in Williston just in the last year. It's the fastest-growing town in the US. I live in a village that was always just 300 people. I've a sixteen-year-old daughter and 150 men have just moved into the village. How do you think I feel about it?' David, who I run into whilst looking for the remains of Evans's dwelling just outside Stanton, North Dakota, is relaying the dizzying speed of expansion of the new oil boom here.

It's true: everywhere we turn there seems to be a fracking oil well, with a huge 100-foot naked flame burning off the residual gas (which, if harnessed, would also be a considerable source of energy) from massive holes in the earth. Everyone I encounter talks about a new satellite photograph of North America at night. Where North Dakota used to register as an empty black space, since the boom over the last five years this rural state now beams up a source of light pollution to rival Los Angeles and New York, a testament to the open flaming sores that plague these north-western counties.

House prices are rising fast, forcing out many rural people to the nearest large towns, but the few who have hit oil in their garden are secure for now. For a handful of fortunate farmers at the nearby Fort Berthold Reservation, who formerly toiled to grow crops on difficult land, it's a sweet turnaround to be wealthy overnight – particularly given the difficult times that the Three Affiliated Tribes (Mandan, Hidatsa and Sahnish, who live on the reservation) have been through since John Evans's day. The lasting environmental damage to the ecosystem and water table could be catastrophic, but in the stark reality of the moment many willingly take the gamble to frack.

David hooks me up with the park rangers who look after the museum at the site of the Knife River villages. It was here, near the confluence of the Knife and Missouri rivers, that the Hidatsa and Mandan tribes lived in clusters of hundreds of earth lodges – until 1837, when the population was once again hit by a devastating small-pox outbreak, this time reducing their numbers from over 2,500 to as few as 153. The old round village dwellings now resemble a series of lunar craters, and archaeologists drool at the seemingly endless churning to the surface of artefacts, crockery and bone that the burrowing, mole-like pocket gophers dig up – free of charge – when it's not frozen over hard. (Today it's minus 20 degrees Celsius and we are clothed in layers of Arctic-ready quilted garments.)

Big White's (Sheheke's) village, beside where John Evans lived in his log home, is now buried under a gravel pit next to the gigantic coal power station in Stanton, near present-day Deapolis. The sense of scale of the earth lodges is lost, dwarfed by a mile-high smoking chimney, but back at the Hidatsa Knife River site it's easier for us to imagine how the village would have looked, and we can speculate soundly that Evans would have walked here too.

But now it's time for lunch, at the fancifully named Café du Monde in Stanton, where the words:

Live

Laugh

Love

are hung on the interior wall in twisting wrought-ironic letters.

Curly fries all round.

TWELVE

AN IMAGINED
WINTER WESTERN

The raising of the Spanish flag

Now begins a new chapter in the John Evans story, one that resembles a great untold Wild West adventure, but is set in the snowdrifts of a quasi-polar vortex. Evans is the intense, principled and lonely protagonist, working diligently for the Spanish crown, who recites the Bible to himself in a strange tongue when alone in his increasingly wretched, newly occupied wooden fort: a glorified log cabin.

His host tribe, the Mandan, are the good guys who have saved his life with gifts of food, shelter and company, and it is they who will save his life when the bad guys (in this case the British Canadians) turn up to try to kill him and retake the fort. (You could probably throw in a love triangle for effect, but as previously noted this would be based on speculation alone.)

Evans plays a lonely whistle on occasion and enjoys the spectacle of a Buffalo Dance. He works on his maps and journals by candlelight, and, when invited into the lodges of his host tribe, makes persistent enquiries through an interpreter as to what lies beyond the prairies to the west, and whether they have ever encountered a tribe of pale-skinned warriors who speak a foreign tongue.

The film is slow-moving, and its two-hour length takes us from early autumn, through a dark winter, to the sweet thaw of a Great Plains springtime (spectral dawn scene of white-tailed deer leaping through the long grass as a cuddly plains grizzly bear licks its paws clean, ready for the emerging day), in a conveniently seasonal composition. It's way better and way bleaker than the Marlon Brando-starring movie *Missouri Breaks*, even though its cast are all newcomers.

Evans now takes over the English/British/Canadian fort . . .

On 28 September 1796, he writes in his journal:

. . . in Conformity to the orders I had, I took possession of the English forts belonging to the Canada traders, and I instantly hoisted the Spanish flag which seemed very much to please the Indians . . .

The crazed audacity displayed by Evans in this instance is underlined by the historian Professor James P. Ronda, who writes in the introduction to the Bison edition of A. P. Nasatir's *Before Lewis and Clark*: 'With more daring than good sense, he seized the trading house and planted a Spanish flag firmly over it,' adding, 'His northern plains sojourn was perhaps the high-water mark for Spanish exploration on the Missouri.'

Coincidently, back in Europe, Spain and Britain were about to go to war. On 6 October, war was officially declared. Evans and his small band of French-speaking river-men were in sole colonial charge of the 49th parallel, one of the longest borders of the Spanish Empire – though, of course, it was the Mandans and Hidatsas who were really in charge. The unexpected emergence of Evans from the south and his breaking of the Lakota and Arikara blockades must have caused great curiosity within the Mandan and Hidatsa people, but he was welcomed warmly by his host nations, and they continued to treat him jovially.

Evans's political decisiveness, meanwhile, had shocked the Canadians, but he was resolute. He sent his first Canadian visitors away with a copy of James Mackay's declaration for their superiors, and documented the incident in his journal:

The 8th of October arrived Several men at the Mandaine Village belonging to the Canada Traders . . . they had brought some Goods, not having a Sufficiency of men I did not strive to oppose their arrival, nor of their goods: I nevertheless found a means to hinder their Trade and some days after absolutely forced them to leave Mandane Territory, I sent by them in the North the Declaration that I had received of Mr. McKay: forbidding all strangers whatever to enter on any part of his Catholic Majesty's Dominions in this Quarter under any pretext whatever —

The declaration in question was addressed: 'To all British Subjects Trading to the interior parts of N. America, and all other persons of whatever description who may frequent the said Country.'

This unexpected decree set off a flurry of cross-border diplomacy and correspondence. The rival Hudson Bay and North West trading companies across the border in Canada took different tacks. Desperate somehow to hold on to one of their most abundant trading partners, the Mandan nation, James Sutherland of the Hudson Bay Company maintained a cordial tone through these tense wartime exchanges and expressed interest in developing a friendship with the most interesting (and isolated) Evans, sending him gifts of magazines and chocolate with every correspondence. Cuthbert Grant, representing the North West Company, had a shorter fuse, however.

These early months were a honeymoon period for Evans, who was held in high esteem by the Canadians. He had even given one of the traders from the North West Company his own compass and the company of one of his own men when he politely turned him back to Canada. Relations soon turned cold enough, however. Evans had expelled from his own fort a French-speaking Canadian by the name of René Jusseaume, who was an employee of the North West Company, and although he would emerge as a historically significant character, this experienced fur trader of the wilderness had a reputation of being rather a loose cannon. Even worse for Evans, Jusseaume had married a Mandan woman and had children at the village. His personal anger towards Evans was soon to become very real. As this tense cold war developed, the seasons were changing too. Snow returned to the prairies, and Evans settled in for the winter in close proximity to his generous hosts, the Mandans. He would gain from them, he hoped, all the information he needed to discover the source of the Missouri for his maps, and to plan his route to the Pacific Ocean. He planned to set off in springtime. Last, but not least, he hoped to verify the Mandans' origin as the Madogwys and, should this not be the case, to find clues to their whereabouts from his genial hosts.

THIRTEEN

ICE FISHING WITH
CORY SPOTTED BEAR

Driving towards Twin Buttes from the south on Highway 8, under grey skies, we cross the border into the Fort Berthold Reservation and take a right at the crossroads on to Highway 22.

A speed violation on this road would still get me, an outsider, a North Dakota speeding ticket, but if you're a member of the Mandan/ Hidatsa/Sahnish nation of affiliated tribes who control this reservation as a near sovereign state, then you're no longer under state jurisdiction, so you get an appointment with the Tribal Council instead.

It's freezing cold. I mean minus something or other: icy bristles stick up from every surface like metal shavings on a magnet. Our truck stutters to a halt in front of the elementary-school building.

'I own the only burgundy pickup in town,' Cory had told me on the phone. 'My house is right by the school. You can't miss it.'

I've already spotted three burgundy trucks within a hundred yards of the school, all parked in front of uniform wooden houses. 'Burgundy', the Word Jazz song by Ken Nordine, starts to play in my head. I press 'Pause' in my mind's ear and phone Cory again.

Out he comes from one of the houses, waving. (He owned the truck I thought was least likely to be his.) He is a most welcoming man and invites me in for a coffee (John's still asleep in his bunk).

His eagle-feather plumage hangs on a coat rack. Deer antlers and home-made flutes and pelts are on the walls, there's a flat-screen TV, and Pendleton and home-made First Nation rugs are on the sofa.

Cory is a fit-as-a-fiddle 36-year-old of Mandan, Hidatsa and Norwegian descent. His left leg was paralysed by West Nile virus at the age of twenty-seven, not that you'd know it, as he's more agile and outgoing than most people I know.

'I'm an outdoor kind of guy,' he tells me as we head through a side door into his garage to get the gear.

A few days earlier, when I was passive-smoking outside the Japanese restaurant in Bismarck, I had met a guy from the reservation who knew Cory well. 'He's an outdoor kind of guy,' he told me. 'They used to call him the gunslinger before he was paralysed, just from the way he used to walk square, hands hanging six inches from his body, like this.'

Back in Twin Buttes, we are packing the pickup with all we need for ice fishing:

One gas-powered ice drill (a metre long, red)
One ice saw
One tent
Two stools
One spear to catch the fish
Two small fake fishes to dangle and entice the walleye and pike

The van packed, we head into the mountains above Lake Sakakawea, on a twisting, snow-covered road. Here we pass a turning to a lakeside gated community of summer homes owned by the Corps of Engineers, where the local people are not allowed to go, let alone build their own houses.

There, from atop the ridge, we look down at the majesty of this curse of a reservoir. Cory explains what we are looking at: 'All the best lands were under here. Our people were pushed up into the barren mountains, where nothing grows easily. John Evans was so lucky to have spent time with our tribe here at the height of their civilization.'

Yet Cory Spotted Bear is not a bitter man. Descending towards the lake, he's looking to the future and making sense of the present. He sees the terror in my eyes as we leave dry land and he drives the pickup out on to the frozen 178-mile-long reservoir.

We drive around until he has figured we're above around seven feet of water, then we stop and unload everything from the back. Together we drill a hole through the ice, widen it into a TV-screen-shaped hole, push the tablet of ice into the lake and behold the magical yellow light of Sakakawea's waters as they come into view.

We erect a tent so that the fish below don't realize the ice is broken, and then sit inside, on our stools, dangling our fishing lines through the hole, Cory with spear at the ready. Then we talk and talk.

When he was eighteen, Cory tells me, he took the advice of his grandmother and his aunt and sought out the knowledge of tribal elders. He took a particular interest in Edwin Benson – the last first-language speaker of the Mandan language and also a fine singer and storyteller. His aunt, Alice Spotted Bear, forewarned him: 'Be respectful around him, he's weary of people bugging him all the time for his knowledge – academics keep turning up. Be patient.'

But he persevered and gradually persuaded Edwin to share his precious language and songs with him. He started to rediscover his own history, having only been taught about Lincoln, Washington and the greats of US civilization at Halliday high school; he now discovered the history of Black Cat and the Cory Bears. 'We kind of become displaced through our forced change, and assimilation – "kill the Indian, save the man" – was the policy, so my generation, we're coming back from that,' he says.

Cory also studied plumage-making with elders, and traditional flute playing with Keith Bear. Finally he taught himself how to build a traditional Mandan and Hidatsa earth lodge, now seen as the epitome of sustainable architecture. He plans to build an entire village in the mountains above Twin Buttes, where he and his friends will move their families and live in circular homes laid out to a traditional circular plan. The exteriors will resemble the old earth lodges and merge into the landscape in a turtle-like hump. Inside, however, there will be Wi-Fi and the latest technology, all powered by wind and solar energy.

'This is the obvious conclusion of how our tribe should be living in the twenty-first century, respecting the land like we always have whilst making the most of the technologies we are given. If he lived today, Black Cat would have certainly used the gas-powered ice drill!' Cory tells me, laughing.

BOBCATS

After a two-hour conversation, staring all the while into our hole in the ice, we are yet to catch anything, apart from a cold. A turtle swims up to say hi to Cory, we are introduced, then she moves on.

'I need to check my bobcat traps,' Cory says. 'I've been learning to set traps in the old way.' He looks at the time on his phone. 'We'll need to stop by my aunt's house to pick up the snowmobile.'

We pile everything back into the pickup, draw a few circles on the ice with the tyres and head back to the shore. Up the hill we go, stopping briefly to watch a herd of white-tailed deer run and bounce away from us.

On the third peak we reach a house perched on a cliff. The icy lake shines a mile or two in the distance and a few hundred feet below.

Cory gets the snowmobile out: it's a 300-dollar burgundy 1979 Yamaha. I jump into a kind of sledge that's tied to the back and we head at full throttle down a steep incline. I almost fall out, but quickly learn to lean into the mountainside as he turns.

After a mile or so, in a secluded valley, we stop at a beaver dam. An incredible sight, though any water here is frozen over, of course. The traps are empty (having been turned on to vegetarianism by The Smiths as a teenager, I'm pretty relieved), but I realize how thorough Cory's thought process is towards his role in his surroundings.

He explains that he lets most animals go, keeping only the aggressive males that pose a danger to the community, and that when he replaced the fast food of his formative years with a traditional diet, a number of his pretty severe ailments disappeared. He now kills his own meat, hunting buffalo at a controlled reserve twice a year.

The snow deadens the valley's acoustics, and I feel absolutely at peace: there's only the sound of coyotes and birds, and Cory over there fiddling with the traps.

Then we jump back on the snowmobile.

'Let's go see Uncle Edwin,' says Cory.

FOURTEEN

AN IMAGINED WESTERN
CONTINUED . . .

The battle for the border

Winter closes in on our isolated protagonist. The honeymoon period is over.

As the flurry of correspondence by courier between Evans's Mandan village home and the Canadian trading forts over the border continued, the developing story was documented in the journal of the Hudson Bay Company's James Sutherland. René Jusseaume's relationship with Evans, meanwhile, was to be severely tested.

On 26 October 1796, James Sutherland wrote:

Wednesday. Snowy weather . . . a party under a Mr Evans a Welsh Gentleman, who has come to explore the source of the [Missouri] *River as far as the stoney* [Rocky] *Mountains if not to the Pacific ocean in search of mines, some of which is already found, Mr Evans permitted him* [Hudson Bay agent] *to return for this time without confiscation of his property, but on the promise of not returning again with any goods.*

Representing Canada's North West Company, Cuthbert Grant had some exchanges with Evans that were also cordial to begin with:

Mr Evans

Sir,

*I . . . beg you will be kind enough to deliver the bearer all the
property of any kind belonging to . . . Gousseaume* [Jusseaume] *that
may be in your possession, he has wrote to you himself to that effect he
is to pass some time here himself to settle his affairs but means to return
to the Missisourie in* [the] *course of next month.*

> *Sir*
> *Your most obedient*
> *Humble servant*
> *Cuthbert Grant*

Evans, who was now living in Jusseaume's fort, which he renamed
Fort Mackay, had developed an increasingly austere tone in his correspondence with his Canadian counterparts. In response to a particularly
neighbourly if highly inquisitive letter from James Sutherland, he
dryly maintains:

. . . Having no entertaining news of any kind to transfer to you,

I remain
Dear Sir

Your Obt Servt.
J. T. Evans

By February, Evans, living in what was often minus 20 degrees
Celsius conditions (temperatures can drop to minus 40 degrees Celsius
in North Dakota – minus 10 is a decent winter's day) in a European-
style log hut rather than one of the better-protected earth lodges of the

villages, was running out of supplies. And according to the gossip of the Canadians, revealed in James Sutherland's journal, his health had deteriorated. He was, it seems, in a bad way all round. Having expected that reinforcements and supplies would have arrived from Fort Carlos at the Omaha nation, and having himself promised an array of goods to the Mandan Chief Black Cat, Evans was facing a severe crisis.

Meanwhile, half a continent away in New Orleans, Mr Andrew Todd, who along with the Spanish government in Madrid was the financier of the whole Missouri Company expedition, had succumbed to yellow fever and was by the end of 1796 in a swampy Louisiana grave. The expedition, in short, was screwed. Evans was cut off from his superiors, and Mackay was now in retreat from the Omaha, aware that the whole Spanish enterprise in North America was in peril and that the steady stream of supplies that was needed to placate the insatiable Chief Blackbird of the Omaha was now drying up. Evans was the most isolated European in the Americas. But, as ever, nothing could deter him from his responsibilities. On 25 February 1797, James Sutherland wrote in his journal:

Saturday . . . About 3P.M Slettar and Yorkston arrived from the Mandals with 4 sleds well loaded with furs, Mr Evans was as cival to them as his wretched sitewation would admit, but would not permit them to Trade with the Natives, he Traded all the goods they had and gave them furs for it, but would have bought it much cheaper had they dealt with the natives . . . Mr Evans hoisted his Spanish Flagg.

In the face of increasingly aggressive communications from the British, Evans, under the guidance of his host tribe, continues to plan his journey west. The seventh Evans-derived chart at the Beinecke

Library contains the first depiction of the Yellowstone River on a map, and covers the area to the west of the Mandan lands along the Upper Missouri River to the falls of the Missouri and further west to the Rocky Mountains themselves. Crucially, Evans depicts the Rocky range for the first time as a three-tier band of mountains. Evans's Mandan and Hidatsa guides, who traded and fought with the Shoshone and Crows to the west, had helped him to form a more realistic vision of the geography and challenges that lay ahead.

The pestering from the north, however, continued to distract the freezing Evans. Following yet another failed attempt to trade with the Mandans directly, and the loss of two horses to a stray hunting party, an angry John McDonnell from the Hudson Bay Company wrote to Evans on 26 February 1797, openly questioning his credibility as a Spanish representative and accusing him of employing Canadian deserters as his foot soldiers and even of bribery.

[. . .] *British subjects are not to be tried by Spanish laws, nor do I look upon you as an officer commissioned to apprehend oth*[er] *people's Servants, if you serve a chartered Comy* [company] *why not show the Spanish Governors Orders, declarations, denounciations or manifestoes, prohibiting others from frequenting that Country – Then we shall leave you in peace* [. . .] *most certain I am* [of the belief] *that there is most complicated vilainy carried on this year at the Missouri* [. . .]

Dr Sir Your Very Humble Servant
John McDonnell

Still worse was to come. Jusseaume had now reached the end of his tether with the crusading Spanish Welshman Don Juan. Indeed, our imagined John Evans western movie now reaches its most severe crisis point . . .

Back on my investigative concert tour, I go on to write a song about the test that Evans is about to face at the hand of Jusseaume, the Canadian. I visit a recreated Hidatsan earth lodge at the national-park site outside Stanton to make a demo recording, as it has excellent acoustic properties. Once there, I light up the open log fire to battle the brutal cold of the North Dakota winter, and hit 'Record' on my Korean palmtop. It's a work in progress, but here are the lyrics from Evans's perspective, which I sing, accompanying myself on guitar. Avatar John sits back on a colourful cotton rug that has been placed upon a large pelt, and maintains his elderly demeanour throughout.

SUGAR INSIDES (IN THE KEY OF A)

You come down from a' Canada,
With a letter for the king.
You staked a claim on a territory,
An assassin's mind within.
My trusty interpreter gave me clues of my demise.

You've got to sugar inside the gun,
You've got to sugar inside the gun;
Sugar the insides,
Keep trouble outside,
For a future beyond the gun.

You had to wait till my back was turned,
You're a coward and a cheat!
You filled your pistol with deer-shot,
And stood upon your feet.
You took an aim towards me,
But my friends, they dragged you out.

You've got to sugar inside the gun,
You've got to sugar inside the gun;
Sugar the insides,
Keep trouble outside,
For a future beyond the gun.

They said that they would kill you,
So I challenged you to a duel.
You turned me down and then fled the scene,

Oh! Jusseaume, you fool.
You ran across the border,
You could say I saved your life.

You've got to sugar inside the gun,
You've got to sugar inside the gun;
Sugar the insides,
Keep trouble outside,
For a future beyond the gun.

Or, in the words of John Evans himself:

13th March 1797

*Arived at the Mandanaine Village from the North, a man named Jusson
[*Jusseaume*] accompanied by several Engagees* he was sent by the
English traders, with Merchendizes as presents for the Mandaines and
neighboring nations, so as to be able to break off the attachement and
fidelity they had promised to his Majesty [*the king of Spain*] and his
Subjects, the said Jussom and those who Accompanied him advised the
Indians to enter into my house under the Mask of Friendship, then to kill
me and my men and pillage my property; several of the good chiefs who
were my friends & to whom Jussom had offered presents; refused them
with indignation and shuddered at the thought of such a horrid Design
and came and informed me of the Whole. Nevertheless the presents that
Jussom had made to the Indians had tempted some inferior class, who
joined him to execute his abominable Design, happily for me his*

---

* Soldiers of French origin, hired for a specific period or purpose. Many of Lewis
and Clark's men were also considered *engagés*.

presents had not the same Effect with some of the Principal chiefs, to undertake Such an enormous crime, therefore many of those chiefs Came to my house to guard me and were resolved to die in the attack should it be made; this resolution disconcerted entirely my enemies and totally put an End to their infamous Design. Some days after Jussom came to my house with a number of his Men, and seising the moment my Back was turned to him tried to discharge a Pistol at my head loaded with Deer Shot but my Interpreter having perceived his design hindered the Execution – The Indians immediately dragged him out of my house and would have killed him, had not I prevented them – this man having refused me Satisfaction for all the insults he had given me, Moreover disgusted at the ill success of the Execution of his Black Designs, left the Mandanes with his men some days after and returned to his people in the north [. . .]

Evans had, with the unwavering support of the Mandan chiefs, resisted the attack. And his offer to Jusseaume of a gentlemanly duel was the final straw for the experienced trader, who returned to the North West Company's fort with his tail dragging behind him in the snow.

Evans's next journal entry confirms that he was well aware of the geopolitical significance of his presence on the northern borders. It's more than possible that he had an inkling that the momentum of US expansion would eventually engulf his seemingly distant post. Indeed, within a decade his location would signify the northern border between the apparent revolutionary, egalitarian US and the royalist colony of British Canada. As he elaborates in his journal:

I found out by all I could learn that the Intentions of the British Traders were Not to spare trouble or Expense to maintain a Fort at the

Mandaine Village Not that they see the least appearance of a Benefit with the Mandanes but carry their views further, they wish to open a trade by the Missouri with Nations who inhabit the Rocky mountains, a Trade that is at this Moment is Supposed to be the best on the Continent of America [. . .] The best Quality of Land is found in the Mandaine country, this quality of land extends itself on the West as far as the East chain of the Rocky Mountains which are about 170 leagues to the West of the Mandaines, it is at these Mountains where the Meadows and Prairies terminate the Country then begins to be Absolutely Covered with trees, even upon the Rocky Mountains and it is probable these trees extend to the Pacific Ocean.

Spring was coming, and if he was serious about reaching the Pacific then Evans would soon need to pack up, travel west and see these trees with his own eyes.

FIFTEEN

DOUGHNUTS WITH THE LAST SPEAKER OF MANDAN

I t's dark as we drive to the top of the ridge in the burgundy pickup. We turn off the road down a short driveway into a courtyard that has two one-storey wooden houses either side, but there's a lot of stuff there: pickups, cars, horses, chickens and farming paraphernalia.

A simple wooden archway bearing three sets of deer horns crowns a small gate in front of Edwin Benson's house, the smaller of the two dwellings. After 200 years of aggressive assimilation policies, two major smallpox outbreaks and two forced repatriations of the tribe, Edwin is the last speaker of the Mandan language.

Two of his granddaughters are playing *World of Warcraft* on a gigantic screen in the living room, which the front door opens on to. We walk past the back of the sofa that houses these make-believe warriors and go into the kitchen, where Edwin and his daughter welcome us warmly with coffee, fried chicken, doughnuts, mini-pizzas and cake. Mandan hospitality is legendary: it's no wonder that Evans survived his harsh winter here and thought so much of the people.

A new foal was born this morning, so 82-year-old Edwin has been pretty busy, but he also found time to drive to Washburn, an hour away, to do some shopping.

'Grandson,' says Cory Spotted Bear. 'How are you?'

'Pretty good, Grandpa,' replies Edwin.

'Grandson, these people are from Wales.'

Their interaction sets my mind spinning, and I have to remind myself of the Mandan tradition of turning linear time on its head so that the elder becomes the child, and vice versa. This prepares me for a conversation in which I will be consistently required in the warmest possible way to suspend any preconceptions I have about history, evolution and myth.

Edwin explains that he is the keeper of one of his tribe's sacred 'bundles'. The Mandans' medicine is the turtle, and the sacred bundles are partly made up of three centuries-old turtle-shell-like drums, the remains or representations of what are believed to be the originators of the Mandan people (four original turtles came from the river, but one escaped back into it and is communicated with by tying fabric and objects to a willow tree). These sacred bundles are distributed amongst the clans to chosen 'Carriers'. After a weak Carrier member of the tribe sold one of the sacred turtle drums to a Washington gallery in the last century, the tribe had to work really hard to get it back. When they succeeded, Edwin's grandfather, Buffalo Bull Head, or Ben Benson, who also raised Edwin and passed on to him his language, then became the keeper of this bundle. He passed it to his son, and when Edwin's father died, Edwin received it. Since the Washington debacle, the sacred bundles are not to be viewed by the public and are used only in a real emergency as a prayer tool, in the presence of a tribal member, for example if one of them is unwell.

'And that leaves me in a funny bind,' says Edwin, who is a practising Christian. He points out the paradox between following his own Christian belief in what he considers to be a 'jealous God' and the cultural responsibility he has in protecting the sacred turtle and the ceremonial practices of the Mandans. It's the kind of burden that only a cool head like Edwin could handle. And it's by no means his only burden in life, as Edwin is, for now, the last fluent speaker of N'ueta, the Mandan language.

'Mandan language was my first language,' he explains. 'Then, later on, when I started school in 1936 or 1937, I learnt how to speak English. I couldn't speak Indian in there; they wanted you to speak English. And if you made a mistake by talking in Indian in school, you got punished for it, and each time the punishment got a little stronger.'

In Wales the school punishment until the very early years of the twentieth century was famously the 'Welsh Not', whereupon the child who spoke in Welsh would have an engraved *WN* sign hung around their neck. This was passed on to the next culprit, and whoever wore it at the end of the day would be beaten with a cane. 'They don't make that soap any more,' says Edwin, referring to the punishment used in his own schooldays. 'I've never seen it [since], but I know the taste of P&G soap that they made me wash my mouth with for talking the Mandan language. I still don't speak very good [English], but I got to learn, and if I talk to someone for business I know enough to get the point across in English. But in Mandan language I can rattle it off like nothing, you know.'

I ask him whether there were other children speaking Mandan when he was at school.

'Very few,' he replies. 'The Hidatsa language was the strongest where I was going to school. It's still used. Over in Mandaree, there's a lot of them that speak that fluently, but there's no one round here that speaks Mandan now. He's the one that's learning to talk Mandan now; he does real good,' says Edwin, gesturing at Cory with a piece of chicken.

I tell him that I learnt English by osmosis, from watching TV, and that my first English word was 'cookie', after the Cookie Monster in *Sesame Street*.

'Cookie, huh?' comments Edwin, looking at the steadily decreasing plate of doughnuts in front of me.

Edwin has a quick sense of humour that belies the cultural bookend that he represents. Of course, he did not know he would have the responsibility of being the last in his line to be able to recite his clan's and his tribe's histories in his father's tongue. (His mother was Sahnish.) His first wife spoke a Lakota language, so they passed on Lakota and English to their children.

When he was twenty years old the authorities started to build the Garrison Dam, which destabilized the existing Mandan-speaking community even further, forcing them to move apart and into daily contact with English-speakers. Mandans of school age were sent to boarding schools designed to rid them of their mother tongue, and those of Edwin's friends who could speak Mandan gradually passed away. How quickly a language can fade over time, and with it a whole range of idioms, forms of knowledge and cultural practices, developed over millennia, which offer the keys to living in a certain way. Mandan, like most languages, has grown out of the landscape, its surroundings, its weather and people, and it's a true tragedy when we lose something that helps us to understand the earth we stand on.

'Cover your ears, I'm loud!' laughs Edwin. His granddaughter has left her *World of Warcraft* game for a second to bring him his hand drum, which is about the size of an Irish bodhrán or an extra-large pizza.

'OK, this song used to be called "Women Dancing". The men would sing this song and the lady would go and pick a dancing partner, a brother-in-law or a grandson or whatever – one that she can tease and stuff. That's the rules they had in them days. So it'd be mostly the women picking the men to dance with, and they would sing a song like this here, you know.'

He bangs his drum forcefully, and a huge, beautiful voice of yearning blooms out of his body. This is followed by a Lakota number, a song by a boy from the Rockies and a Mandan oldie written by a blind songwriter, plus a 'doorway' song. Doorway songs were sung by groups of young men who would walk through a village, stopping occasionally to gather by the doorways of young women to serenade or playfully tease them in song. These are very old songs, designed to be listened to rather than to dance or go into battle to. I sing some Welsh numbers from my chair, behind my diminishing plate of snacks, and then it's Cory's turn. It's my best night out in years.

'OK, well, there's a song that my grandson wants me to sing,' says Cory, 'and that's a song that I was able to create because he's teaching me the language. This last song is a song that came from the star spirits. I don't need a drum for this one – this is from the stars.'

As Cory sings his beautiful song a cappella, we all look down solemnly in respect, just as we did for Edwin's tunes. Then I get to join in the fun again, with some more unaccompanied songs of my own in the Welsh language.

I ask Edwin about the supposed connection between the Mandan people and Wales.

'Wales?' jokes Edwin. 'I've never heard of Wales – makes me think of those big sea creatures.'

This time of reflection in the friendliest of kitchens, high up on a snowbound hill, makes me dwell on the language that I grew up speaking – itself at a crossroads. Obviously, the suffering endured by the Welsh pales in the light of the still-recent catastrophes endured by the First Nation American tribes. Still, there are parallels with European minority languages that hold.

In Wales, with roughly half a million native speakers left, we have an incredible opportunity to rescue our language. But it will take a consensual, determined political effort, and a radical, strategic overhaul of education and planning policy, and quickly, if Welsh is to stand any chance of survival. Otherwise, at the current rate of change, a rural kitchen ensemble could be the destiny of the Welsh language too. Luckily for us we still have a choice, but with many heartland areas falling under the 50 per cent level of speakers in the 2011 census we must be aware that we are at crisis point and this extremely special offer will not last for much longer. Let's hurry up, while stocks last.

Of course, John Evans, being John Evans, had a very different strategy for cultural survival. He saw all this coming in the eighteenth century, which is why he ended up here in the upper Missouri, on one of history's most unusual reconnaissance missions, desperately attempting to facilitate an exodus of his people to join the tribe of the Madogwys.

SIXTEEN

THE BIG THAW

AND THE

VAPORIZATION OF

JOHN EVANS'S DREAM

Plus a final instalment of the western within a western

Our imagined western movie now enters its climax. Spring is nearly upon us, and the tense diplomatic scuffle with the Canadians and the various threads of the narrative so far, from the Spanish financing disaster to the quest for the descendants of Madog, now come together in a definitive conclusion.

On 14 April 1797, James Sutherland wrote in his journal:

. . . News from the Mandals, Mr Evans and The Canadians almost at fisticuffs in attempting to prevent them from trading with the Natives, and not having goods himself set all the Indians out against him, he [Evans] *was obliged to set off with himself and all his men down the River for Fort Charles* [Fort Carlos], *The Indians threatening to kill them if they refused being greatly exasperated against them for preventing the subjects of G. Britain from coming to Trade with them.*

Evans's supposed departure was premature gossip from Sutherland, but the game was now truly up for Evans. Manuel Gayoso de Lemos had replaced the very supportive Francisco Luis Héctor de Carondelet as governor of Spanish Louisiana and had reinterpreted the provision that the Spanish crown would cover the expense of maintaining the forts along the Missouri to the tune of 10,000 pesos. This was now expected to come directly out of the Missouri Company coffers. With the financier Andrew Todd lost to yellow fever, and internal bickering between Todd's partners in trade Jacques Clamorgan and Governor Zenon Trudeau disrupting proceedings further, all of Evans's colourful promises of a steady supply of goods from St Louis to Black Cat's Mandan nation were proving to be empty. The resources of the Missouri Company were spent.

The Welshman with the golden tongue, who had talked himself from an isolated mountain village to the distant metropolis of London, then across the Atlantic Ocean, down the Ohio River, up the Mississippi, out of jail and 1,800 miles up the Missouri from St Louis, was now five years into a hugely ambitious solo expedition, to which he had devoted himself completely. But for the very first time he had to consider turning back.

With his newly gained knowledge of what lay to the west, he would have realized that it was an impossible journey even to contemplate without further supplies of goods and equipment. He was stranded in the Mandan villages, and as the snow and ice thawed, and springtime returned to the pristine wilderness of the northern prairies, reality and John Evans finally met and shook hands.

Despite all the cultural coincidences that tied the Welsh to the great Mandan civilization – the leather and wicker coracle-like river boats, the tale of the Lone Man, and the earth-lodge villages that resembled the Iron Age forts of Tre'r Ceiri – Evans was forced to abandon his youthful romantic instincts and become a realist: an experienced man of the wilderness. As the first surveyor of the great river, he encapsulates his experiences with the nations of the Missouri in his journal:

As to the manners and the customs of the Indians I found they differ little one from the other. In the different parts of the continent across which I voyaged, all I could remark was, that the nations who had but an imperfect knowledge of the Whites (Being yet in a state of nature) were of softer and better character.

During his incredible journey from the East Coast into the American interior, he had lived with numerous tribes and had met representatives of further tribes that lay thousands of miles west in the Rockies. They in turn traded with tribes who lived in the deserts of the south-west. But none had ever encountered a tribe of Welsh-speaking, pale-skinned warriors. Evans awoke from the innocent delusions of the Welsh intelligentsia and entered a new, hallucinatory reality: Madog was dead, a figment of the medieval imagination. Evans's half-decade journey had been in vain. Iolo Morganwg's persuasive impassioned speeches had been nothing but a crude imperial fantasy. Evans was devastated.

Enraged, shamed and seemingly stranded in an impossible situation, he informs Chief Black Cat of his plan to return downriver, to investigate what has happened to the promised goods of the Missouri Company, telling him that he will come back with both guns and supplies. Black Cat agrees, and in May 1797 Evans turns his back on his dream for the first time and aims his thawed-out boat downriver, harnessing the full force of the great Missouri to descend the rapids towards Fort Carlos. The almost suicidal speed at which he now rides the current of the churning river down its snake-like bends mirrors Evans's swirling psychological descent into the plughole of a dark depression.

SEVENTEEN

LOST FOR WORDS
AT THE
4 BEARS CASINO

Running Elk, Marilin Old Dog and Keith Bear explain all

Finally we make it to the capital of the Fort Berthold Reservation, New Town. This is where the council of the Three Affiliated Tribes meets. There's a high school and, just beyond on the hill, the Three Tribes Community College, one of a network of tribal colleges spread across many of the reservations of America, a by-product of the political activism of the 1960s and 70s, when the boarding-school assimilation education system that had helped to destroy the morale (and the mother tongues) of the tribes was finally and firmly rejected. The mostly single-storey buildings are packed down with icy snow, making this small town appear like a collection of sparkling white boxes on this blue-sky day.

We stay the night at the 4 Bears Casino, where you can still smoke indoors and where the restaurant serves a reassuringly high-fat meal well into the night. Oil men and women, but seemingly mostly men, gamble everything in high-stakes escapades before drowning their sorrows at the bar, or quietly shed tears as they punch holes of frustration into the veneer walls of the adjoining hotel rooms, where the rumble of a touring country act can often be heard, vibrating in the brass fittings. The winners celebrate with a spree at the gift shop, then appear heroically drunk at dawn, sporting replica feathered headbands.

The following morning, John and I eat a variety of cooked eggs, then head to New Town's high school for a 9 a.m. concert. A patient class of older students awaits, along with some significant community elders, including the musician Keith Bear and the museum curator Marilin Hudson.

I'm still a bit groggy, but John is charm personified in his felt hat and humours the young audience with his undemanding presence.

It's a vivid experience, as I'm suddenly addressing a class as if I were a teacher, albeit a singing one, making use of the class globe to explain Evans's journey, and projecting my slideshow on to a screen. I play a few numbers, including my '100 Unread Messages', with a new verse bringing it to the present:

Up with the Mandan,
You raised the Spanish flag,
Survived assassination,
Worked upon your maps.

My early-morning show and PowerPoint presentation pass uneventfully into memory as we drive over the gigantic concrete bridge that spans the western end of the Sakakawea Reservoir, heading for the JC Java Coffeehouse. We were warned in Bismarck not to expect fancy coffee at the reservation, but the opposite is true in oil-boom New Town. If we're talking about the centre of industrial America's fossil-fuel-speculation universe, then we're right at the heart of it. You can get anything here. And we are here for information. We down our caffeine shots and walk the snowy pathway to the tipi-shaped modernist museum where we hope to solve the quandary as to where and how the supposed link between the Welsh and the Mandans was formed.

Here we meet with historian Calvin Grinell, who is passionate in his quest to arm us with a truthful representation of tribal history. He was one of the generation of the Three Affiliated Tribes who were sent away to boarding schools in distant states. He left to join the Marine Corps, another rite of passage for the contemporary warrior, but, sense of identity developing, he adopted a tribal name and in 1983 took part in the first Okipa ceremony to be held since they were outlawed in 1890. As he was a warrior's age, the skin of his chest was broken with the hanging hooks, and he fasted just as the warriors used to do back at the Knife River villages in John Evans's day.

Grinell now works for the Tribal Historic Preservation Office of the Three Affiliated Tribes in New Town, here on the shore of the Sakakawea Reservoir, which flooded the Class 1 soil of the banks of the Missouri at the Fort Berthold Reservation in the early 1950s, displacing its residents to the less fruitful uplands on the opposite side of the narrow, man-made lake. This means you might now have a 100-mile journey to see a relative or a former neighbour if you have to drive around the lake. There are many parallels with the flooding of the Treweryn River in Wales in the 1960s, which displaced the residents of the Welsh-speaking community of Capel Celyn, sparking a radical uprising of political activism nationally – although the scale here on the Missouri would be unimaginable back home. This reservoir would span the length of Wales itself.

As a rigorous historian, Grinell is suffering some fatigue from the many attempts over time to find links between the Welsh and the Mandan people, a link that John Evans thought he had proved to be fictitious, but which was revived over and over again through the nineteenth and twentieth centuries by luminaries such as the artist George Catlin, Prince Maximilian, and an array of Celtic romantics, still fanning the tall tale of Madog that persists as *real* history today in some Welsh and American circles.

THE VÉRENDRYE DOCUMENT

Grinell believes he has pinpointed the source of the idea that the Mandan tribe were pale-skinned and had fair hair, galvanizing the belief that it was the Mandans, out of all the tribes in America, who were the likely descendants of Madog. He calls his document 'Vérendrye's Mistake' (after the French explorer Pierre Gaultier de Varennes, sieur de La Vérendrye) and produces a copy for me on a simple one-sided piece of A4 paper.

In his document, Grinell quotes Vérendrye's biographer Lawrence Burpee:

> He [Vérendrye] was persuaded, from what the [Assiniboine] Indians said that they [the Mandan] must be either whites or an unknown race enjoying a degree of civilization far beyond anything found among the other Indian tribes . . . La Vérendrye, when he actually visited the Mandan, somewhat unreasonably reproached the Assiniboine with having willfully deceived him . . . They [the Assiniboine] replied that they did not mean the Mandan when they spoke of a nation like us, that they meant the nation that dwells down the river and that works in iron [i.e. eighteenth-century European settlers].

Operating as part of a vast tribal trading network across continental North America, Grinell believes that the Mandans and Hidatsas – and even their rivals, the Assiniboine, to the north – would have been travelling into areas of European occupation to the south and encountering European traders for many years before the first official European visits. The eyewitness account Vérendrye obtained from the Assiniboine chief actually concerned real-life European settlers that he saw during a long journey south from his tribal home in what is now Saskatchewan, Canada, not an indigenous tribe of blue-eyed, white-skinned North Americans. This, however, was lost in translation. When Vérendrye finally entered the Mandan villages in 1738 as the very first European documented to do so, he saw no trace of people with pale skins, but the myth had already been born and carried all the way to old Europe, and once it entered the minds of the eager Welsh, nothing could stop its momentum.

THE LUNCH BUNCH

Later that morning, the legendary flute player Keith Bear turns up to take us for lunch with Marilin at the Three Affiliated Tribes Community College canteen. A musician and storyteller with both Mandan and Sioux blood, Keith was 'raised as a Mandan boy'. He has previously toured in Wales, where he stayed with a vegetarian folk-singing family, so he's not too miffed when I don't join him and Marilin for their speciality, the lamb soup (another cultural coincidence). And even though sharing the same food would be good manners, it's a cheese sandwich for me and John, who after a few weeks of eating at Midwestern truck stops has also become a vegetarian.

After lunch, driving back through the icy roads of New Town past the oil trucks and the tribal souvenir shops, Keith tells me that the reservations were originally divided up into different sections and given to evangelists from different Christian denominations to come and build churches. As a young boy he was initially excited by the prospect of becoming a polygamous Mormon, but in time his spiritual side gravitated to that of his Mandan ancestors and their understanding of the Earth.

He also has a tribal name: 'Among the Mandan people my name is Bright Light That Waves in the North Sky. In English, my name is Northern Lights, and Northern Lights is only a reflection. I'm a reflection of my family, I'm a reflection of my clients, I'm a reflection of my tribes, my communities, my reservation, my state. When I go to your country, I'm a reflection of America, so I have a great responsibility in my name. So, everything I do reflects; everything you do reflects.' His words are purposeful and effortless.

We are heading now to an earth-lodge village, built just out of town past the casino, on the glistening frozen lake shore. In the middle of the village there is a giant earth lodge which acts as a lecture hall, theatre and powwow hall. The Okipa ceremony would have taken place in an earth lodge like this, and it's here that Keith Bear wanted to bring us to hear his flute songs. We exit the car and look out at the iced majesty of the Missouri waters of the Sakakawea Reservoir, and the hills beyond. The sun brings out the inner light of the snow, creating an idyllic otherworldliness. Underneath, however, from Keith's point of view, is a darkness, as fracking and industrialization encroach on the formerly abundant wildlife.

We make our dotted lines of footsteps in the crisp snow, from Keith's car into the great hall of the earth lodge. Keith Bear unearths his collection of flutes from a bag made of traditional woven fabric; all the flutes have either been carved by himself or presented to him as gifts. He tries them out for our benefit.

'So I have many, many friends of different colours, and some of them, they don't understand our language very well, some don't speak English and I don't speak their language, but we have a

communication – the flute – and so the flute is a thing that talks,'
he explains whilst weighing up his flute options.

The most impressive-sounding is a twin-barrelled one, which plays
two notes at once.

A gifted, self-taught musician who started singing late in life, Keith
is also a natural storyteller. When I ask him what his take is on John
Evans, his words flow like the mighty Missouri itself:

John Evans? When he travelled here it was
good, because our lodges back then
provided him with a home for the winter
time. Our gardens fed him good food and
good strength over that winter and good
medicine for the wounds of his heart and
his body and the healing of his mind, also.
When he came here he was following a path
of another man that they say came this way,
Prince Madoc. So our people have been
discovering each other and meeting each other
for a very long time along this river.
And I think it's very important that we
continue this connection and find this way
of keeping this bond together, because even
though we are on the other side of the
world, our connections politically and
geographically are quite similar, physically. Our lodges are considered very
similar to the stone lodges of the Welsh
people. Our bull boats are very similar to
the conical boats that they have there in Wales.

Some of their food is very similar to ours, and they
say some of our words are very similar also. So,
whether there's a myth or whether there's a
fact, I think it's important that we as human
beings continue to encourage our children to
look into our history. You can see that we are the
people, the Mandan, the Hidatsa. We still exist and
we still thrive.

Here in this lodge, this is where we share some of
our spirituality, this is where we share some of our
culture, this is where we share ourselves, with those
who travel from far and wide. So, for you to come here
and to enter our lodges – to enter our families and to
enter our community – it's more than just coming
to take a picture. You represent your people. You
will take back the things that you see here, what you
feel here, what you're giving here, what you share
with here is as good as what John Evans shared so
long ago. In 1792 he landed, and it was a few years
after that that he came up here to these very
shores, to the very water that we drink and live
on today, so that we can carry our culture, share
the culture of the music and the culture of our
medicine, the culture of our ways, the culture
of our spirituality. And maybe some of your
children will come here, maybe some of our
children will go back over there, maybe
some of our children will become related.
So that's what we hope for a good world
of tomorrow.

You see, John Evans
must have had some kind of spirit,
to leave his home, travel halfway
across the world on a ship that wasn't
nearly as good as what we have today for
sailing the seas. To travel across America,
where it takes us a few days to drive, it took
him months to walk. For him to look for food,
to face the animals and the adversity that he had
to face in those days, was very, very great, but
his spirit was strong, his spirit guided him. His
upbringing, those who taught him how to provide
and how to look up and how to get along, those
people were very strong. And they inspired that
young man. That gave him the strength and
the courage, and so that's what we try to teach
our children too – to have that kind of
strength. And that spirit that comes from
the animals like our buffalo stories, our
elk stories. These are very strong
animals, and we use those virtues. It's
a spirit that was instilled into your
relative, John Evans, so long ago.
He was following a mythical
person, Prince Madoc. Was he
real? John Evans thought so.
Who knows, but now you
know that your relative was
here, and we were glad to be a
part of his story and to carry

on those things that will encourage our children. You
see, it doesn't matter what you look like on the
outside, it's what you have on the inside that we
use to help to communicate. That's what a
warrior is about among our people.

A warrior is someone who helps in a communication – not just to go out and destroy and to hurt other
people – and a warrior earns the respect of those around
him. John Evans must have had a lot of respect, because
when he left here, they told stories about him for a long
time. And now here you are, hundreds of years later,
honouring him. We say 'remembering with honour',
and that's what you're doing: remembering with
honour your relatives.

This young man came from a place where they
have a very strange-looking animal on their flag;
it's a combination of the air and it's a combination
of the earth, and it's a combination of the mythical
stories as well as real things. And that's what we
do too: we bring our animals to life; we bring our
stars to life. Everything around us in this universe
gives us life. And so for that young man to tell us
stories about his dragon people that came from
far away, to hear our stories of the things that
we have in this water and the respect that we
have for our stories in the stars. Those stars
help guide us and those stars help protect us,
and the stars – we say some of them are
relatives who have gone before us, passed
on to the next world.

By the time we leave the lodge, the day has departed. There's a clear night sky, and as I look up from the icing-sugar lake, I imagine a John Evans built of stars, pacing out into the sky, southward-bound. It's time for us to leave too, and to follow the pathward made for us by Evans as he turned back for the first time, his dreams of finding Madog's lost civilization in pieces, but a new, unimaginable knowledge of the Mandans' and Hidatsas' civilization gained. I imagine that this was the defining moment of his life: free at last from the filter of mythology, yet now confronted by the blinding crystal-clear light of a new and treacherously icy path.

The lost tribe was a lost cause,
So you cried a silent tear,
And fled back to St Louis,
To a familiar frontier.

ACT THREE
VOID IS INFINITY

PRINCIPAL CHARACTERS

MANUEL GAYOSO DE LEMOS

Governor of Spanish Louisiana (New Spain), 1797–9.

KELLEY TODD EDMISTON

Present-day New Orleans tour guide and the daughter of a voodoo priestess.

DANIEL CLARK

Eighteenth-century New Orleans merchant, connected to the Missouri Company.

THE LETTER

N ow is a good time to read John Evans's letter to Samuel Jones, written following his return to St Louis from the Mandan nation, recapping his journey since leaving the Jones household in Philadelphia four years earlier:

St Louis July 15th 1797

Dear Sir

It is such a long time Since I have departed from your part of the world that I am ready to suppose every body of my friends in that Part of the world has given me up for dead. However after innumerable escapes from red and white people and [having] *undergone some of the severest hardships I suppose was ever experienced – I am – by kind providence preserved to have the pleasure of informing you as well as my other Friends of some particulars of my Travells. After I left your house I Proceeded to Fort Pitt where I was kindly treated by a certain gentleman of the name of Dr C Wheeler for a month to wait for the high waters. From thence we was transported in a few days to Limestone in Kentucky. From there I travelled by land to bourbon and from there through the wilderness to Cincinata – here I was kindly received by General Wilkinson. Stayed here a few days – then departed for Louisville and from thence for New Madrid in*

Louisiana. Here I was kindly received by Mr and Mrs Rees my country-people – but was obliged to take the Oath of Allegiance before I could be permitted to debark – now begins my life of misery and hardships – in 10 days after my arrival was taken by a violent and Intermiting fever succeeded by a delirium – Thank god for friends for I was paid the greatest attention to in my sickness by my kind land lady and all the Great People of the place, otherwise I should have died in the greatest Poverty – Having undertaken the Voyage of discovery up the Missouri upon the Strength of my own Pockett which consisted of a dollar and three quarters when I left your house – in 2 months my fever abated a little, my resolution and anxiety for proceeding on my voyage being heightened to such a pitch that I was determined to risk my life, feeble as I was, and start to the Illinois in Company with one man only. Neither of us knew the road – if it could be called a road, for it was so overgrown with grass that in several places not the least trace was left – however such as it was, we had the bad fortune to lose it altogether in the evening of the first day – Now lost in the infinite wilderness of america – Oh unsufferable Thirst and hunger is an amusment in Comparison to this – The parent sun who is so much courted by the northern nations has in this distressing moment turned my Enemy and threatens to beak my brains like a cake and withdraw from me my Pressuous Eye Sight – 3rd day here my fever returned and my Eye Sight recovering – Came to a country overflowed with water. Travelled several miles in water from the hip to the Arm Pitt amongst a numerous Crowd of the biggest water reptiles I ever saw – The 7th day arrived at Virgen a Spanish Post in the Illinois. The night before, we slept within 5 miles of this village – but on account of my weakness which kept me unable of Travelling above a hundred yards without rest, it took us all day nearly to get to the Village – in a miserable situation, I arrived bear foot, bear legged and bear headed. Here stayed a day to rest myself – next day went to Kaskaskia on the American side of the Mississippi where I was kindly

received and treated by John Rice Jones Esq, another countryman – here
my fever turned nervous and I have been several days neither asleep nor
awake. I arrived the same year as I left Philadelphia in the later end of
July. Stayed here 2 years to wait for a passage up the Missurie – but that
country being under Spanish Government and Engrossed by a Sett of
Indian traders I had no prospect till Christmas 1794 when I was informed
of a gent at St Louis who was engaged to go up the aforesaid River for
three years. Now or never, as I thought, it was my time to make
application – so I went over the Mississippi. I thought within my self that
it was rather a ridiculous busyness as it was a Critical Time on Spanish
side on account of the report of Clark's armie and I not able to speak one
word with any body, they speaking French – however, I went and was
taken for a Spy, Imprisoned, loaded with Iron and put in the stoks besides
in the dead of winter. Here suffered very much for several days till my
friends from the American side came and proved to the contrary and I was
released – In August 1795 I started from St Louis in Company with James
Mackay Esq, Comandant of the Missurie – wintered with him the same
year at the nation Mahas on the Missurie – here I started with the Indians
to the hunting ground, with whom I stayed 25 days and returned to the
said Post Maha where I stayed 2 months[. I]n Februrary 1796 started on
my voyage to the west but at the distance of 300 miles from the mahas was
discovered by the Enemy the Sioux and obliged to retreat and returned to
the Mahas[. I]n June following undertook the same voyage and arrived
safe at the Mandans and Bigg Belly nation 300 leagues from the Mahas
and 600 from the confluence of the Missurie with the Mississippi –
Description of the country 2600 [sic] leagues from St Louis is a woody
country[. W]here the Missurie runs through is a bottom from 12 to 18
miles wide[. T]he Missurie in its turns touches some times the hills on the
north side – the general run is under the south hills – for 400 Leagues it is
full of Islands and receives several Considerable Rivers from R. Platte 190

*leagues from St Louis – To the Mahas the Missurie glides along in as
curious turns as any River in the known world Through a fine meadow as
level as a Table 18 miles wide from one hill to the other – a traveller often
imagines in going up that he descends the country on account of its curious
meanders* [. F] *rom the Panias* [Pawnees] *to the Mandans 190 leagues, the
Missurie by furious and revengefull Power in some far antient time has
bursted its way through the mountains – and miny hills.*

    *Thus having explored and charted the Missurie for 1800 miles and by
my Communications with the Indians this side of the Pacific Ocean from
35 to 49 Degrees of Latitude I am able to inform you that there is no
such People as the Welsh Indians – and you will be so kind as to satisfie
my friends as to that doubt full Question – in July 1797 I arrived at
St Louis after the long voyage of 2 years up the Missurie* [. W] *as well
received by the Officers of this Place but I suspect that I shall be obliged
to undertake other voyages as dangerous as the former as there has
already Solicitations been made to me by government to undertake a
voyage across the Continent, which voyage I suppose will keep me from
having the pleasure of Seeing you as I think but very little of a trip to
Philadelphia at present, having been so far up the Missurie that it took
68 days to come down with the furious Current of the Missurie.*

    *Dear Sir, present my best respect and friendship to Mrs Jones and Miss
Sally but I suppose I may call her by some other name by this time.*

I am, Dear Sir, with due respect your very humble servant

J. Thomas Evans.

On 9 May 1797 John Evans plunged in retreat down the Missouri
River. With no resources left, he would have been wholly dependent
on the generosity of the river tribes, who knew him well by now and

let him pass through their villages. When he arrived back at Mackay's base of Fort Carlos in the Omaha Nation, he would have found a deserted wooden fort. There were no more resources left for Upper Louisiana from the Spanish Empire. There was talk by the new governor of Louisiana, Manuel Gayoso de Lemos, of sending up a gunship from New Orleans to ease the river travel of the Missouri Company, but it never got further than St Louis, such was the expense of maintaining an armed militia for a long period of time.

Evans sped downriver in his boat, past the fort and, according to A. P. Nasatir only sixty-eight days after departing from the Mandan villages, he arrived in St Louis, on 15 July, 1,800 miles down the Missouri River basin.

Once there, he chronicled his whole journey from Philadelphia in his remarkable three-page letter to Samuel Jones, the bulk of which was extracted by Morgan John Rhys in articles concerning the non-existence of the tribe, published in the *New York Daily Gazette*, the *Philadelphia Gazette* and the *Philadelphia Aurora*. How painful that last page would have been to write: to declare publicly to the world, and especially to the Welsh, that the myth of Madog and his descendant tribe was, indeed, nothing but a myth.

Evans had devoted his entire being to finding a tribe that had never existed. Frozen, broiled, bitten and battered, his mind and body had been thoroughly pulverized by most of the elements and climates known on this Earth. Even after jail terms, attempts on his life and hellish diseased interludes, he always carried on pushing for the ultimate goal: to find the Madogwys. Now this had been taken away from him, what remained? How would this daredevil adapt to an adrenalin-free civilian life?

Initially there was still the tantalizing promise of revisiting his Pacific quest. He had passed his Missouri test beyond all expectation, given the wretched circumstances, and seemed poised to receive another calling from the Spanish, should there be another expedition. But this wasn't to be. The political power of Spanish Louisiana in New Orleans was weakening, and the coffers had shrunk. Defending what they already had – from the Americans, British and the rebel French of Northern Louisiana – became a more pressing concern than funding an uncertain exploration of the unchartered lands of the Rocky Mountains and the Pacific North-west beyond.

Governor Zenon Trudeau, despite having always been rather sceptical of Evans, nevertheless decided to reward both him and Mackay for their success in surveying the Missouri and repelling the British threat to the northern borders, not to mention their canny diplomacy with the nations of the Missouri. So Mackay became the commandant at San Andrés, Missouri, whilst Evans received the post of official surveyor for the Spanish government under Antoine Soulard, beginning on 9 November 1797, at the town of Cape Girardeau on the western shore of the Mississippi, in what was to become the state of Missouri. Evans was instructed by Trudeau to keep his eyes peeled for a location to stake a land claim of his own, and, as he left his friends in the St Louis and Cahokia area and moved downstream to a new life of potential relative wealth, this must have seemed a promising time.

But, as often happened, the reality of adjustment for this soldier of the frontier was to prove difficult. When he returned to the sweaty cauldron of the Mississippi swampland, there was a marked deterioration in the usual enthusiastic, even boastful, tone of his early correspondence. In a place where his rudimentary language skills in Spanish and French put him at a disadvantage and where hard-knuckled frontier characters jostled for land grabs, the methodical gringo surveyor assumed the position of an unpopular disciplinarian referee at a sporting match.

Or so it seems from the logistical documents relating to his time in Cape Girardeau, within which lies some correspondence that shines a light on his life and the increasingly desperate deterioration in his morale. It is not recorded, but one wonders whether he had heard through his network of Welsh acquaintances of the death at Lampeter of his brother Evan, to whom he was close, of tuberculosis at the age of twenty-four. What we do know is that John Evans had in all probability been attacked and robbed of most of his possessions, including all his clothes, except those he was wearing. Creditors were not paying up, and the 28-year-old struck an aged melancholy tone in a letter to Trudeau when petitioning him to grant him land he had surveyed in Hubble Creek in Jackson, Missouri:

A reflection upon the shortness of life, and the frowns of delusive fortune – convinces me dayly of my duty to live a retired life as soon as I can – For we can scarcely mount the stage of life – Before we ought to prepare to leave it to make room for the next actors[*. I*]*n a solitary life a man is allowed a few moments to converse with himself while in the crowd . . .*

All was not lost, however, and in a letter to Monsieur Soulard he notes, 'In probability I shall become an inhabitant of this post and have a family perhaps before long.' Did he have anyone in mind? He certainly did make some friends during his time in Cape Girardeau, where he lived in the Cape La Cruz area of the town. Beyond his social life he also made a lasting impression on the town plan, and according to an essay on Evans by A. P. Nasatir in *The Mountain Men and the Fur Trade of the Far West* (Vol. III), edited by LeRoy R. Hafen, 'The names of many of the land grants that were surveyed by Evans are still extant.' Whilst the street names and even some buildings have persisted, alas, sickness was endemic in these wretched swamplands, and Evans lost most of his friends to it.

Unsurprisingly, he made another Welsh friend in the wilderness, this time a southern Welshman, Maurice Williams, a neighbour in Cape La Cruz who obviously saw Evans as a fixer and a confidant. After Evans returned briefly to live as the guest of Jacques Clamorgan in St Louis in July 1798, Williams wrote to Evans in Welsh, asking for help in finding him a polite, intelligent wife, preferably a 'widow or old maid . . . about 30 years of age', adding that he trusts Evans to find him a good match.

Evans also maintained contacts with his American friends, including one Mr A. Weston, who pines for Evans in his letters, much as Mackay did for him in their Missouri days. Evans was still, it seems, a charismatic presence, even as he deteriorated in the swampy funk of New Spain.

Eventually Weston ran away from his creditors in Spanish Louisiana, but tantalizingly mentions in a letter to Evans that he has left 'Evans's book' with a Mr Howe at Fort Messac. Could this be one of Evans's missing journals? We can only speculate, but what is certain is that Evans's work for the Spanish – maps, journals and observations concerning his Missouri expedition – was received by Mackay, who, as Evans's superior, incorporated it into his own work and presented this under his own name to Gayoso de Lemos, the governor of Spanish Louisiana. Indeed, in Mackay's petitioning letter to him on 8 June 1798, he seems to take sole credit not only for John Evans's cartography, but also for his campaign to repel the British from trading in the future Dakotas, even though Mackay wasn't there:

I also found means to drive the English out of his Majesty's territories &
took possession of a fort which they built at the Mandan nation . . . I also
took a chart of the Missouri from its mouth to the Wanutaries [Hidatsa]

nation which following the windings of the river is a little short of 1800 miles . . .

But perhaps this was just a general musing on the successes gained under his leadership. Governor Gayoso de Lemos certainly knew of Evans's achievements, and there's nothing otherwise to suggest that Mackay undervalued the role of his friend.

In October 1798, once the intensely abundant vegetation had receded for the autumn, Evans suggested a return to surveying in Cape Girardeau, but the land he had petitioned for had already been earmarked for another by Monsieur Lorimier, his commissioner at the Cape. With international tension rising, the threat of war between the US and the French was causing American immigration into Louisiana to slow to a trickle, meaning unsteady work for a surveyor. Coupled with Spain's paranoia at the threat of a British invasion from Canada, which Evans had temporarily repelled, he had good reason to visit Louisiana's capital, New Orleans, to petition the governor directly for work. Indeed, it turned out that Manuel Gayoso de Lemos had plans for him:

It is very important to divert [drive out] *the English from the Missouri, all the more so, since that is the only way to prevent them penetrating into the Kingdom Of Mexico, which otherwise would be very easy for them . . . Forseeing the importance of the matter, I tried to keep to our cause the two most famous travelers of the northern countries of this continent: one Don Jayme Macay and the other Don Juan Evans, both natives of the Island of Great Britain who . . . entered the service of our Missouri Company. But when this company failed due to its poor management and great losses, I knew that necessity would oblige these two valuable subjects to solicit employment among the . . . Canadian companies to our very own great loss. In order to*

avoid this inconvenience, after having Mackay at my side for some time to
assure myself of his principles, I have decided to locate him at San Andrés . . .
naming him commander of that post . . . Not having any position to give
Evans I have preferred to maintain him at my cost, keeping him in my own
house, in order to prevent his returning to his own country, or for his own
convenience embrace another cause.

So Evans was off to New Orleans to live in the most comfortable
open prison imaginable: the house of the governor, whose occupier
didn't want the young Welshman to stray too far with his precious
knowledge of the interior. Furthermore, Spain was due to appoint an
astronomical commissioner (surveyor) to take part in discussions
concerning the northern border of Louisiana with his American and
British Canadian counterparts. Gayoso de Lemos, who had already
been appointed to represent Spain as a separate commissioner for
boundaries, was now petitioning the Spanish government directly for
Mackay and Evans to play a leading role in a highly significant survey
of the Canadian and Mexican borders, and the eventual ratification of
a treaty with the US and the British.

The future, despite Evans's severe setbacks, seemed to point in
the short term to an unlikely and esteemed existence under the Spanish governor in New Orleans, but far ahead Evans glimpsed the
promise of a glittering career as an acclaimed sculptor of international boundaries.

ONE

TURN BACK IN ONWARD

*A potted journey with Avatar John
from the Canadian Border to New Orleans*

It's heartbreaking to leave New Town and the Fort Berthold Reservation: the welcome and generosity have been so warm, the conversations and the songs so inspiring, the political outlook so familiar. John Evans, too, would have felt as if he were leaving home.

We drive south through the rugged upper Badlands of Highway 22, past the Hidatsa stronghold of Mandaree towards Killdeer and Dickinson. The giant naked flames and hydraulic arms of the oil wells, together with rock formations worthy of a western movie, compete for our tourist's gaze. After a day we pass from North Dakota into South Dakota and contemplate a detour to Devil's Mountain, just across the border in Wyoming, famed for its depiction in mashed potato in *Close Encounters of the Third Kind*. We glimpse real-life drones training for Asian assaults, and pass by the nuclear missile silos and magnificent, other-worldly Badland Rocks, just north-east of Pine Ridge Reservation and Wounded Knee. The snow has melted down here; we cross the unfrozen winding Missouri at Oacoma and wave out of the window towards our friends at the Omaha Reservation and the Bright Eyes crew in Omaha City. But the excitement we had previously felt when searching out the new has evaporated. We're just speeding down a familiar concrete highway in the other direction, to fulfil our commitment to play shows in Memphis and then New Orleans.

Before that, it's yet another day's journey in the truck back to St Louis and a quick stop for a Ted Drewes Frozen Custard to battle the heat. Plus we need to investigate Cape Girardeau properly. This is taking us days, man! John's clothes are beginning to look a bit scruffy, with felt fuzzing up on the arms.

In Jackson, Missouri, where John Evans had hoped to claim his land and settle down on Hubble Creek, we park up in the Walmart car park, not that far from the very spot, then head up to the Trail of Tears state park to camp the truck above the glistening valley of the Mississippi for a night under the stars. Once nearly 50,000 Choctaw, Seminole, Cherokee, Muscogee Creek and Chickasaw, as well as African American slaves, were walked like cattle in a forced exodus, with much suffering and death, along the Trail of Tears, which took them westward to Oklahoma, from the Deep South and the Carolinas.

In beautiful, quaint Cape Girardeau, which Evans helped to survey, name the streets and populate with new migrants, we meet a grouchy old man. Faced with our enthusiasm for the Mississippi, which runs parallel to the main drag of coffee shops and antique stores, he dismisses the whole goddamn river. 'That thing?' he says, pointing at the great waterway. 'It's just an open sewer.'

Memphis beckons. We marvel at the reflective-glass quasi-pyramid structure of the Pyramid Arena. The nineties-era conference centre is under reconstruction and will soon become the world's biggest fishing-tackle and gun shop. We are booked to play the Hi-Tone bar on Poplar Avenue, formerly Master Kang Rhee's karate studio, where Elvis famously used to practise his moves in relative anonymity (and where he received his eighth-degree black belt in 1974). The building is still owned by his former karate master, and a photo of the two of them has pride of place behind the bar. Backstage a dark humour prevails. Printed signs decorate the rooms. A warning to staff reads:

ALL GEAR, PERSONAL ITEMS, AND ANY OTHER SHIT YOU LEAVE UP HERE FOR LONGER THAN 2 WEEKS WILL BECOME PROPERTY OF THE HI-TONE. TAKE YOUR FUCKING SHIT HOME.

A general diss to anyone who happens to be reading signs (in this case John and I) hangs on the dressing-room wall and states in a Southern accent but with no uncertainty:

FUCK Y'ALL

Otherwise, the ghostly 'Elvis died for us', rock and roll, karate vibes feel pretty good in here. The show brings in some beautiful, kind music fans, who in some cases have travelled from inner Arkansas. We give it our all and try to catch a conversation with our fellow travellers as they exit the venue, but we have some pressing matters to attend to: not only is the paranoia of being in the most intensely seismic point in North America magnified by the humidity, but we also have a rendezvous with the Devil. We pack up the equipment at 10 p.m. sharp, jump in the truck and speed down the Mississippi highways towards Clarksdale, to attempt a meeting with the ultimate myth of modern American music: a recreation of the midnight rendezvous of Robert Johnson with the Devil at the crossroads of Highway 161 at Clarksdale, Mississippi.

Obviously Johnson never actually met the Devil, as Radiolab pointed out in its great radio documentary *The Crossroads*: it was that other bluesman, *Tommy* Johnson, who met him. This misinterpretation derives from Pete Welding, a 1960s student and blues nut at UCLA who wrote a widely distributed article about Robert Johnson, having misheard one David Evans relaying the 'Tommy Johnson meeting the Devil' story. Robert Johnson, coupled with this new mega-myth, then became an international retro sensation, kick-starting a huge blues revival in long-haired Europe, with the likes of Keith Richards and Eric Clapton leading the way. As we have seen ourselves, a myth can get completely out of hand.

We show up in Clarksdale at exactly midnight. I crouch down with John next to the Delta Donut bakery and try out a new number called 'The Swamp'. But the Devil never shows up to tune my guitar. It doesn't help that the so-called crossroads is, technically speaking, by now a traffic island. The Delta laudably refuses to conform to its blues clichés. Indeed, when the writer Will Hodgkinson attempted the same meeting a few years ago, some guy, possibly the Devil, showed up at midnight in a baseball cap and suggested he took more guitar lessons. In any case, I continue to strum my guitar, and play 'The Swamp' again, just in case.

> The swamp,
> It pulls me,
> And cradles me down.
> The heat
> Destroys me,
> The deathbed foul,
> The road has no more turning,
> The yearning breaks,
> We fall together,
> The heartbreak takes.
> But I'm not scared of dying,

I'm only scared of making you cry,
And I'm not want for trying,
I'm just a tourist passing you by,
I'm just a passenger waving goodbye.

We eventually give up and park the truck at a vacant motel front to await daylight. Even though sweaty and exhausted from our cross-continental drive, we are still more than excited about our next show, in New Orleans.

We plan to take the scenic route down the west side of the Mississippi valley via the juke joints of the Delta to Natchez, the pearl in the shell of colonial Spanish architecture, but the climate's changed again. A flash flood has engulfed all the levees, and no matter where we attempt to cross the mighty river – and we try every minor road, seemingly, in the whole state of Mississippi – the roads are closed and we must turn back. Our three-hour jaunt becomes a twelve-hour journey. At one point we reach a tiny village called Onward, which seems to consist of a closed gas station and a couple of houses, and even here, we see to our amusement, the road ahead is closed and we have to turn backward, but not before learning it was in Onward in 1902 that President Theodore 'Teddy' Roosevelt refused to shoot a bear that had been designated for him to kill on a hunting trip. It was a matter of principle: he wanted to hunt and kill his own bear. It was this saved bear – caricatured in the *Washington Post* as a cute bear that was too pretty to shoot (even though Roosevelt had instructed someone else to kill the bear instead) – that inspired the teddy bear phenomenon.

After driving all day from Clarksdale through the villages of the Delta, it's past midnight and yet we've still only managed to reach Jackson, 100 miles away. But the lure of New Orleans is too much. I pick up some ephedrine pills at a truck stop and drive all night through the moist Mississippi breeze, stopping only once to eat a plate of fries under the awning of a drive-through burger bar as the subtropical rain empties from the sky on to the gleaming electric highway. Soon, powered by gum and Gatorade, I'm ploughing the truck into Louisiana – or at least the little bit that's left of the once-great empire of New Spain, which between 1762 and 1802 ran all the way north to Canada and west to the Rocky Mountains, the land that adopted John Evans and in the depths of whose capital, New Orleans, we are going to try to find out what on earth happened to him before he and Spanish Louisiana itself vanished into the swamp and the footnotes of history.

TWO

MADNESS AND MOSQUITOES IN GIN-SOAKED NUEVA ORLEANS

To experience the heavenly hell of vibrant, cosmopolitan Nueva Orleans in the last days of its Spanish incarnation at the end of the eighteenth century would have been a dizzying and unique malarial pleasure. Perched on a lucky horseshoe bend in the mouth of the Mississippi as it reaches the Gulf of Mexico and the Atlantic Ocean beyond, New Orleans served as a crucial gateway to the French and Spanish colonies of the Caribbean, whose powerful governments initially saw Spanish Louisiana as little more than a backwater breadbasket placed there to feed the booming islands' burgeoning populations. Had they known the scale of its hidden riches, they may have been less casual about its ownership.

The French first established the original 'French Quarter' of the town in 1718, in an area that had been part of an important Native American trade route for centuries, and it quickly drew a multitude of people to its thirteen-block-wide grid, a grid system that remains unchanged since 1721. First Nation traders, Haitians, African slaves, freed slaves, Spanish administrators, French gentry, American port workers, Mexican diplomats, French Canadian fur trappers, sugar traders, gold speculators, convents, bordellos, alligators, snakes, mosquitoes, spiders, yellow fever, cholera, alcohol, processed sugar, raw sewage, tobacco and hemp: all combined in a uniquely intoxicating brew.

Following correspondence written by, or regarding, John Evans we can deduce that by November 1798 he was housed in a comfortable situation at the governor's living quarters on Decatur Street, a few yards from the Mississippi River and a five-minute walk from the Cabildo, the seat of government, located next to St Louis Cathedral. Newly rebuilt after the fire of 1794, the city would have been in good shape, and unlike our experience of following his ghost through the great cities of the East Coast and the Midwest, we can still walk within buildings here where John Evans himself would have spent time.

Governor Manuel Gayoso de Lemos kept Evans on a tight leash

lest he reveal state secrets to the enemy. As the Beinecke Library's maps curator George Miles told me: 'The Spanish in general tried to keep state secrets as close to their chest as possible, so it wouldn't surprise me that they retained him and tried to find some way to keep him occupied as opposed to letting him take that information back.'

An unaccustomed anger born out of the New Orleans heat led him to complain in a letter to his Philadelphian mentor Samuel Jones that Jones had made the contents of his previous letter public, even though Evans had specifically asked him to distribute the news to his friends that there was no tribe of Welsh Madogwys in existence. Gwyn A. Williams notes that he had addressed this letter, dated November 1798, to New York, which indicates that the depression evident in his Cape Girardeau letters had turned into delirium. Williams suggests that 'His spirit broke under the repeated disappointments', and asserts that Evans in his Cape Girardeau period 'began to drink heavily and to lose grip on reality'. This assumption, of course, fits the archetypal paradigm of the Celtic-Welsh tragi-hero. Throughout history and continuing into the twenty-first century, a large number of high- (and low-) profile Welshmen and women have self-destructed. In the second half of the twentieth century, Wales's two highest-profile artists, Dylan Thomas and Richard Burton, drank themselves to a premature death, and at the time of Williams writing in the 1970s, this may have been seen unconsciously as the mark of a truly impassioned Welsh romantic. The fact that General Mackay commended Evans as 'a virtuous young man of promising talents [and] undaunted courage', and six months later we are faced with a picture of Evans that has deteriorated considerably, certainly plays directly into Williams's assertion.

However, the truth may have been more prosaic. Manuel Gayoso de Lemos, writing in a letter to Mackay, reveals:

Poor Evans is very ill; between us, I have perceived that he deranged himself when out of my sight, but I have perceived it too late; the strength of liquor has deranged his head; he had been out of his senses for several days, but with care, he is doing better; and I hope he will get well enough to be able to send him to his country.

Although these are damning words, suggesting that Evans's illness has been brought upon himself by alcoholism, they also recall a previous description by Evans of his (almost certain) 1793 malarial delirium: 'my fever turned nervous and I have been several days neither asleep nor awake'. As W. Raymond Wood has written, malaria 'can recur repeatedly and even kill its victim'. He also believes that 'when Gayoso de Lemos spoke of liquor having "deranged [Evans's] head" he was misreading the symptoms of the disease. A severe case of malaria can mimic mental illness and drunkenness; the more plausible explanation is chronic malaria, not alcoholism.'

In conversation with me, the St Louis historian Carolyn Gilman agrees: 'He seems like a pretty strait-laced guy to me. Everybody has said what a very fine upstanding young man he was and he was so deeply religious, I just cannot imagine that the alcoholism theory is right. Malaria will do that – cerebral malaria will drive people crazy and it makes them appear drunk even when they're not. So I suspect that he had such a bad case of malaria that it was affecting his brain.'

Fellow malaria sufferer Meriwether Lewis was similarly depressed in the vacuum that followed his groundbreaking Pacific trek just a few years later. His worsening condition led to his eventual suicide (although some argue that the root of his illness was syphilis, suffered by many others on the Corps of Discovery expedition). There is no evidence, however, that Evans complained of any of the sores or lesions that would have accompanied this unfortunate disease, so the malaria diagnosis seems more likely.

But for argument's sake, what if we disagree with the madness-by-malaria hypothesis? Could Evans's belief in God have evaporated with his encounters with the magnificent tribes and traditions of the Missouri basin? He certainly toned down his missionary zeal as his journey progressed, though sometimes, with no resources, he seems to have been powered by his faith alone. The boatmen he led up that long river were given portions of liquor daily, a ration he was entitled to himself. Could he have succumbed to alcoholism then on that back-breaking journey? How else did he manage to sleep in sub-zero conditions with little or no shelter? Furthermore, booze was relied upon by malarial sufferers of 'the Chills' (which applied to most people in the then swampy lands of the southern Mississippi). The accuracy of his maps, however, point to a steady hand.

In any case, we can agree that Evans's condition had deteriorated very badly. But nothing could have prepared Samuel Jones for his next letter from New Orleans, sent by the attorney Daniel Clark and dated 3 August 1799. It read:

The enclosed letter from you to John T. Evans fell lately into my hands and I was induced to open it, that by learning the residence of some friends I might advise them of the fate of that unfortunate man who died not long since in this city, after being for some time deprived of his reason. Chagrin and disappointment in his views contributed, I fear, to hasten his end.

He was twenty-nine years old, and had been killed by a cocktail of the Delta's finest blues resources: disappointment, mosquitoes, depression and (possibly) booze. As Carolyn Gilman suggests, 'Evans died younger than most [even then]. And you have to wonder if he died of a broken heart. He'd spent all this time and all this energy and all this effort trying to find these Welsh Indians, and to find that they didn't exist was like taking the purpose of his life away. So what was he going to do with the rest of his life?'

'Yes,' I add, 'and that his life was played out on such a monumental continental scale is unimaginable.'

'Yes,' agrees Gilman, 'on a larger scale than most people's dreams.'

Down in New Orleans,
The church bells did trill,
The body of Don Juan Evans is staying mighty still.
You annexed North Dakota,
You surveyed by the stars,
But here lies your body,
By these disease-ridden bars.

THREE

FRENCH QUARTER
TO FOUR IN THE MOURNING
(SORRY)

---

*In search of the grave of Don Juan Evans with
the aid of the patron saint of the impossible*

S o, as I was saying, the French Quarter of New Orleans that John
Evans would have seen remains virtually intact: still there, still
smelly, still silly, still a tourist trap, but still vital and, more importantly for a person in my predicament, still open late.

It's past 3 a.m. when I point our ten-ton truck into the narrow
colonial grid system. I park up badly along a dark, tree-lined street,
possibly scratching the side of that red car, but I'm past caring. I pick
up John from the passenger seat and walk through the wide-open door
of the Tap Room at the Royal Street Hotel and order a beer at the bar.

A young woman sporting a red Mohican is shearing drunk men's
hair off to my left. Jodorowsky's demented western *El Topo* plays on
DVD through an old television behind the bar, its scenes occasionally
interrupted by blizzards of interference. The bar manager is unhelp-
ful, but the eventual Pale Ale is refreshing in the humidity and eases
the delirium induced by my long drive from Mississippi. At 9 a.m. I
must begin my search for the lost grave of John Evans. And later on

I will play the last concert of the tour. I ponder my schedule, drain the IPA, then carry John back to the truck to rest.

In most cities we have visited on this quest we have been able to arrange meetings with academics, local historians, musicians and political activists in order to squeeze out some rare droplet of information regarding the elusive Mr Evans. New Orleans is different. All phone calls have led down a Louisiana cul-de-sac. Today I am faced with a lonely wild goose chase through the crippling heat of downtown New Orleans.

I start at the Cabildo building on Jackson Square, the capitol building of Spanish Louisiana. The original edifice from Evans's day still stands, modified in the nineteenth century but still there. The Cabildo once housed the office of Governor Manuel Gayoso de Lemos, John Evans's host. Today it houses a historical exhibition of the city. I pester the receptionist. Did Gayoso de Lemos, and therefore Evans, live here too? She's sleepy and doesn't know, but thinks Gayoso de Lemos was buried in the cathedral next door. I'm sleepy too, but also heavily caffeinated, so I jog out of the front door and turn left towards the cathedral. Twenty seconds later I enter the vestibule and am immediately confronted by a plaque in memory of Gayoso de Lemos, who is indeed buried here.

I stalk through the rest of the cathedral, scouring the floor and walls, scanning the multitude of plaques for a sign of Evans. But he's not there. W. Raymond Wood had warned me that no records exist of his burial in New Orleans and that I wouldn't find anything, but I simply refuse not to try. Now it's personal! Evans, poor sod, was sent to extremes by the promise of empire and the exaggerations of John Dee, Iolo Morganwg and countless Welsh fantasists – bastards, the lot of them! Now that I have retraced the epic trail of his unlikely journey, the enormity of his effort and the emotion I feel about his early death are magnified in the oppressive humidity of this tourist trap.

I return to the Cabildo and reacquaint myself with the sleepy receptionist. She, in turn, enlists the help of a passing tour guide, who's leading half a dozen obese, camera-wielding maniacs out of the exhibition space like a mother duck. He's sporting a badge that says:

I ❤ College Rock

This is obviously a bad sign (not to mention unprofessional), but this plaid-aware music aficionado, against all odds, casually throws a firm clue my way as he walks towards the door whilst still guiding his flock through the minutiae of New Orleans historical trivia: 'The governor's house would have been on Decatur – on the site of Café Maspero, I think. It's just around the corner.'

Before I can question him further, the guide has already left. So there's nothing to do except follow his instruction.

Within five minutes I'm walking into Café Maspero on 601 Decatur. The esplanade of the Mississippi itself lies just another hundred yards or so from this street. If you had some freak skill at throwing stones, you could call it a stone's throw away. In the window of the café there's a sign saying:

NOW SERVING ALLIGATOR SAUSAGE
W/FRIES
$9.00 BUN OR PO-BOY

I sit alongside John at the bar. It's a momentous occasion, even if the surroundings are unexpected for a former seat of government.

The café manager, who sports long grey hair tied tightly in a pony-tail, is curious to hear John's story.

'Oh, yeah! If he had malaria he would have been prescribed gin and tonic, no doubt about it – for the quinine content in the tonic water. Let me get him a gin and tonic.'

I feel too much of a pedant to argue the fact that upstairs Evans in all probability had to endure the full force of his hallucinatory fever; quinine was not isolated until 1820, and tonic was not invented for a few decades after Evans's death (and at that on the other side of the world in India), so I decide to relax and enjoy the booze.

Like a professional shrink, the café manager humours the felt avatar and engages him seriously with a firm eye-to-eye gaze as I relay the John Evans story. The multitasking manager places the gin in front of John and gets one for me too. I look around and ponder the location of Evans's deathbed on the site of this very café, presumably upstairs, but in a previous incarnation of the building. I ask the bar manager whether he has any idea of where he would have been buried.

'Well, if he died in 1799 I'm pretty sure they would have buried him in St Louis Cemetery No. 1. It's the only place he could have been, really. You know it's where they shot the acid scene in *Easy Rider*?'

I almost choke on my lemon.

'Oh my shit!' I exclaim, the words coming out all wrong. 'No way!'

'Yes way,' replies the ponytailed bar manager calmly, before adding, 'Unless of course he's under the Superdome.'

The Superdome? Why would he be under the Superdome? My mind races through visions of the aftermath of Hurricane Katrina, when many of the city's inhabitants were forced to shelter there for days on end, juxtaposed with an awkward imagined spectacle of trying to get permission to take a spade in and dig through the Astro-Turf surface of the End Zone in search of my distant relative.

'Well, that was once the site of a most beautiful cemetery, Girod Street. Its remains are partly covered by the dome, and one end of the playing field is haunted, but I don't think it was founded until well into the nineteenth century, so he most probably isn't there.'

That's OK then: I'll happily take the *Easy Rider* option. After tipping my new confidant heavily, I head out into the sweltering mid-morning heat, turn right on to Toulouse Street and walk ten blocks or so north, past the site of the original New Orleans burial ground, St Peter Street Cemetery, and all the way up to the infamous-in-biker-circles St Louis Cemetery No. 1.

The Catholic strain of the Christian religion would have been an absolute religious monopoly during the Spanish years, and anyone not baptized as a Catholic – including John Evans – would most likely have been given an anonymous grave. St Louis No. 1 was opened by royal decree on 14 August 1789, and it was the only working cemetery at the time of Evans's death. But since I've found nothing relating to his burial in the New Orleans historical record – John Evans seeming to have performed his usual trick of vanishing from history – I'm pretty lost as to how I'm going to solve the mystery of the location of his grave. Just as I'm reaching the cemetery gate, looking mostly at the pavement and the crap-coloured laces of my disappointed shoes, I notice a guide bidding farewell to some German tourists. She sees John on my back and walks straight over.

'Well, hello, who have we here?' she asks in an exaggerated actorly voice, her eyes seemingly rolling continuously like symbols on a fruit machine, due to the movement of her arched eyebrows. 'Darling, why are you carrying a voodoo fetish?'

'Oh, no, it's not a voodoo fetish!' I protest. I'm really hot by now and pretty tired, as well as coming down off my gin, so I'm in no mood to engage in conversation. 'It's an avatar of a historical figure called John Evans. I'm his distant relative.' Having just spent the previous hour explaining his tale to the gin pourer, and many weeks relating his story whilst following his journey, I'm seemingly at the nadir of an evidence-free wild goose chase in New Orleans. To have someone bring up voodoo seems like the idiotic final straw. And then I catch her rolling eyes again. They have a strange intensity, unlike any I have ever seen before. She is smiling now at the felt avatar.

'Of course it's a voodoo fetish, dear,' she insists. 'That's what a voodoo fetish is – a representation of a loved one, your relative.'

It's an interesting hypothesis, I realize. So I relax, introduce myself, explain my predicament and outline John Evans's story once again. She introduces herself as Kelley Todd Edmiston.

'New Orleans is very *mañana*,' she states, 'but also very yesterday – in other words, twenty years behind the times – so unless you plan with the right people here, you don't get any information.'

Her parents were music promoters and civil rights activists; her mother moved here from Chicago in 1952, and the 'musicians' wives', as she describes them, eventually initiated her mother as a voodoo priestess.

We walk into the cemetery past the grave of the most famous voodoo priestess of them all, the Voodoo Queen Marie Laveau, who died in 1881. Kelley stops briefly, turns and points. Her hair is tied back into a bun so tightly that it exaggerates the power of her stare. She talks in tangents: 'There was a pit that – you see where the spire is? The spire is above the shrine of St Jude, who is the patron saint of impossible and lost causes – like you and me too, right? That's the yellow-fever church, and the pit where they put the bodies before the church was completed was right there, but if he did die of a disease, whether it be yellow fever or malaria, they were afraid; they would blow off cannons like you saw in the *Gone with the Wind* movie to try and get rid of the bad air. That didn't work, because we now know mosquitoes carry all this stuff, right? And there was a burial pit over there, where they would burn the bodies up to a certain point, then they would scoop it [each one] up, bless it, bag it and tag it, and put it in here, in the Protestant section of this cemetery.'

I'm sceptical, as I know that there was no official Protestant section until the Americans consolidated their power in New Orleans a few years later. Protestants were buried anonymously and indiscriminately here. Kelley detects my unease. 'Now, in 1805, an area at the rear of the cemetery was established officially for the burial of non-Catholics, right? And I know John Evans was a few years before, but still they were building the walls and they were getting this thing [cemetery] off the ground, so he would have been in a section with other people who were non-Catholics. People in servitude who hadn't bought their way to freedom yet and that – plus he knew the governor, for God's sake. They would have done what they had to do; blessed him perhaps at the cathedral. They may have done some burning of something here where the pit was, where St Jude Church is, and then, baboom, [bury him] right there where that tree is.'

We walk towards the tree, past the marble tombs where the *Easy Rider* crew shot the LSD scene of their infamous counterculture film without the knowledge, and to the eventual horror, of the diocese. I'd like to re-enact it with John, but I can barely keep up with Kelley's frantic walking pace. As we walk she tells me that her mother was part of the New Orleans production team, so she, Kelley herself, as a child played around Peter Fonda's feet during the shoot.

I ask her how the authorities kept track of where the many dead were buried.

'The Archdiocese is supposed to keep records,' she replies, 'but sometimes they claim they can't find the exact spot, because during the horrors of yellow-fever epidemics and the malaria deaths every summer, records would get lost, [there would be] floods, fires . . . We're on spongy land still: plumbing and drainage started in the 1850s, but before that time we were literally on a sponge here. Human remains would be scattered around, they would have popped up, they would have tried to cover them over with cement, then they would have put them in tombs. I have no doubt your ancestor is here, OK? That is my belief and it will be backed up some day.'

I'm unprepared for her decisiveness in this matter, but I've little time to process this information as I follow her further and further into the labyrinth of the cemetery, through what seem like canyons of ageing marble shrines, some of which occasionally block out the piercing sunlight. We pass the benevolent tomb for songwriters, which would suit me just fine, and Nicolas Cage's future place of entombment, which resembles a stark, shrunken pyramid, seven feet tall in gleaming white stone, as we go further on, towards a small oasis of green near the back wall where non-Catholics were buried, beyond which the legendary Storyville red-light district used to stand.

Kelley suddenly grabs my arm and shakes me to a standstill. Staring hard into my eyes, she makes a startling declaration that surpasses any expectation I could have imagined ten minutes earlier: 'Your ancestor is here. I know he's here. His spirit's standing between us right now. We're in a very sad place. So we know where that beautiful tree is. I would warrant that in that tree, that live oak, you hear your ancestor – that would be in the voice of the locusts; they're screaming at us from the branches right now. That's him, saying hello to you. OK?'

As she says these very words the volume of the locusts magnifies threefold. It sends a chill of realization throughout my body and drives an intense sensation up the hair follicles of my scalp. I feel scared, elated and physically shaken.

'That tree could very possibly be a couple of hundred years old. He might be under the tree,' she says.

We walk up to it. I place my manifestation of John to sit beneath its branches, then I pick up some pieces of rubble, stone and slate to return to his place of birth in Waunfawr, Wales. Then I join John under the tree to savour the moment and rest a little after our investigative tour of verification. If the records couldn't find Don Juan Evans for us, then maybe voodoo can. I'm an atheist, but this spiritual revelation certainly seems real enough to me in this moment. Kelley joins us, so I ask, 'Does our felt avatar of John Evans fit in with everything?'

'So beautifully,' she replies. 'I would say you have brought John back to life. This is truly a voodoo doll, because voodoo dolls from Africa were fetishes; a fetish is an image of your loved one, your ancestor. None of that sticking-in-pins business – that's bad Hollywood movies. But what you do is you pray to the image of your loved one, of your ancestor who's now in heaven and is a saint or an angel and can intervene for you. That's your loa, so John is your loa.'

'OK,' is all I can say. I'm lost for words. John Evans himself, presumably still a closet Protestant on his deathbed, would likely be horrified by this revelation.

'As it's a voodoo manifestation of John Evans, how should we take care of this doll?' I ask.

'You would light candles, you would have prayer cards, you'd do an altar. Usually a fetish, when it's an African fetish, is much smaller. He's quite big, almost my size, but that's fine.'

I'm beyond delirious. I try to rationalize the situation, and ask Kelley: 'So if we take him back to Wales, we can build a New Orleans-style shrine for him and he can bring a bit of New Orleans back with him?'

Kelley explains further the ingredients of Evans's latter-day life in New Orleans that we must recreate in Wales: 'I think he missed home, but I think he found bits and pieces of home here too; if he went to Congo Square and danced with the free African people who were indentured here, and experienced the Native American corn rituals, heard the music, and because we were such a gumbo and such a rainbow of people and such a mixture of cultures, I believe had he lived longer he'd be more part of our history here too. I have no doubt.'

We make our way back to the road. Sweat is dripping from the tip of my nose and my legs feel like they're made of jelly. My hands are shaking, but the innocent, cute avatar under my arm has become emboldened and emits a heavy presence for the first time on our tour, a tour that seems to have hit some kind of supernatural finality, here at the St Louis Cemetery No. 1.

FOUR

DISPATCH FROM
THE ARCHIVO DE INDIAS,
SEVILLE, SPAIN 2013

John Evans: the Man with the Golden Tongue

Evans was dead in the ground. But just as his body was degenerating into the swamp earth, his maps and notes were being copied out of the notebooks and the journals of the Missouri Company and assuming a new life, passed around and then leaked into the hands of Henry Harrison, the governor of Indiana, who in turn passed them on to Thomas Jefferson, the US president, who in turn gave them to William Clark of Lewis and Clark fame. Another copy of his map was passed on to Jefferson directly by Daniel Clark, who was in effect a US mole in New Orleans and would become its first representative in Washington following the looming US takeover. Upon announcing Evans's death to Samuel Jones, Daniel Clark had written: 'I believe he was possessed of no other property than his Books and Maps of the country which he had surveyed; these latter will naturally remain for the use of the [Spanish] Government.'

Jefferson, whose significance as an expansionist American president is rightly overshadowed by his exploitative excesses as a slave master, claimed Welsh ancestry through his father's family, who are

believed to have originated in Llanberis around five miles as the crow
flies from John Evans's home village of Waunfawr. He was aware of
the Madog myth, and instructed Lewis and Clark to keep an open ear
for any information in this regard during their famous journey.

By the Louisiana Purchase of 1803, when Spain finally ceded the
gigantic land of Louisiana to France, who within the year sold it cheap
to the USA, the revolutionary country so beloved to John Evans
finally occupied the lands where he was buried and whose rivers he
had charted. And had he not guarded its northern borders from the
royalist British?

Kelley was right to claim that Evans would have made quite a mark
in New Orleans, had he survived. He would have been on first-name
terms with the new American governor, the old triple agent Brigadier
General James Wilkinson he had met in Cincinnati. In fact, when
Spain ceded Louisiana they quickly rounded up all the paperwork
that betrayed Wilkinson's true colours, along with any other piece
of paper they could lay their hands on, lest the Americans discover
the hidden secrets of the Spanish Empire. John Evans's remaining
papers, which he so carefully carried with him to his deathbed, including a 1792 letter of introduction by Iolo Morganwg, were thrown
into a box and shipped in a rush to Pensacola in the still-Spanish
lands of Florida in the frigate *Nuestra Señora da las Nieves*. In 1818,
as the Spanish retreated again, they bundled the papers into the frigate *The Peggy* for shipment to Cuba, only for it to be attacked by the
Corsair General Umber under the command of one Captain Francisco
Ruperto of Buenos Aires. The vessel was sacked, boxes were broken
open and many papers thrown into the water. The remaining papers
were held in Havana, Cuba, until it too became vulnerable and the
whole lot – 1,250,000 documents in total – were shipped to Seville,
Spain, to the Archivo de Indias, where they remain today and where

we can still read John Evans's letters in his own handwriting. Alas, most of his journals are missing, as are his original maps. But we can view hand-drawn copies of these by Mackay and Clark at the National Archives in Washington, DC, and the Beinecke Library, Yale, respectively. Assorted letters and papers can also be found in libraries as far-flung as Aberystwyth, Philadelphia and St Louis, and others are very possibly hidden away in some private collection, an untouched archival box or feeding plankton in the deep blue waters of the Gulf of Mexico.

'Yes. That's a real tragedy. Things occasionally show up in archives and maybe some day they'll show up, but I'm afraid it's not likely,' whispers W. Raymond Wood from the screen of my Korean palmtop. 'If his journals are out there, they may be in Seville, but it would take someone a very long time to find them if they were there.'

I ask Carolyn Gilman for her thoughts about the journals. 'If only [more of] the journals survived, he'd be a lot better known today, I think,' she tells me. 'And especially if he'd managed to publish the account of his adventures. Can you imagine what a great book that would have made? It would have been a best-seller, and he would have been famous if he'd just written it down and published it.'

What, indeed, is the legacy of the mysterious, multifaceted John Evans? What are we to learn from his unique adventure? And what were the unexpected consequences of his escapades? Who *was* he exactly?

JEAN EVANS, CARTOGRAPHER

One of Evans's most important historical legacies is the most unlikely consequence of his search for the Welsh-speaking tribe: his emergence as one of the most significant cartographers of the American West.

With seemingly very little training in surveying – just those few months' work at a surveyor's company in Baltimore upon his arrival in the USA and an apprenticeship under Mackay on the first leg of their journey up the Missouri River from St Louis to Fort Carlos – Evans's natural disposition for surveying flourished as he became a map-maker of remarkable accuracy.

'Evans was so important,' Carolyn Gilman tells me. 'He was the first one who actually brought back the information and mapped it scientifically. He shows the Rocky Mountains as a series of ranges, and that was the important thing. Everybody had thought that the Rocky Mountains were in fact just one range of mountains and they're not, they're multiple ranges of mountains. The map that they made after Evans got back [Mackay's Indian Office Map], if you compare it to that [Soulard] map there's just no comparison. That one is basically fictitious – there might as well be dragons on it and sea monsters – but this one is geographically correct and extremely accurate. So that's the difference that John Evans made.'

Regarding the Missouri, W. Raymond Wood emphasized to me: 'Those are the first [eyewitness] maps of the Missouri River, period. And I'm kind of curious as to how he did that, because if you superimpose those maps on modern ones, they're remarkably accurate, down to and including the islands in the river. His maps guided the first full year of the Lewis and Clark expedition out of St Louis – he knew what he was doing.'

And indeed it's realistic to assume that had the Missouri Company's main financier, Andrew Todd, not died unexpectedly of yellow fever, Evans, rather than Lewis and Clark, may well have been the first European to cross the American continent and reach the Pacific Ocean. But he cautiously heeded the advice of the Mandan and Hidatsa tribes, on whose eyewitness reports he based his most westerly maps, and realized that it would be impossible for him to cross the Rockies without further resources from the Missouri Company and the Spanish government. Instead, he created a map for future explorers.

Carolyn Gilman agrees: 'They [the Mandans] probably told him how far it was, and he realized there was no way that he could make it. Lewis and Clark spent the winter with the Mandans, just like Evans did, but it then took them all the next year to get to the Pacific coast. They actually arrived at the Pacific in December of the next year. It would have been impossible for him to make it.'

Of course Evans's malarial madness and premature death abruptly ended a surveying career that could have flourished further, with the likelihood of a direct involvement in the additional surveying of the northern border for the purposes of the Louisiana convention and Purchase (which partly shaped the future construct of North America that still holds today). Combined with the parallel collapse of Spanish Louisiana itself, it conspired to write him and his adopted nation out of history altogether, as when the USA took over Louisiana in 1804 only the events that had taken place in this new period of American occupation were deemed historically relevant. Shadowy figures like Evans and Mackay, who were the heroes of the Spanish occupation, disappeared into the dungeon of history, to be replaced by new actors such as Lewis and Clark.

Gilman corroborates: 'The real tragedy is that it took until about the first decade of the nineteenth century, until after Lewis and Clark came back, for anybody to realize how significant his contributions had been. And then he didn't get credit for it for years and years. It wasn't until historians started looking at his maps in the twentieth century and saying, "Holy cow, those are really accurate, those were scientifically done." I think the people who know the history of the

Lewis and Clark expedition, and know how much was known before then, would give Evans a huge amount of credit. But that's a fairly small part of the population.'

DON JUAN EVANS, SPANISH CONQUISTADOR

According to the Welsh Marxist playwright Gareth Miles, John Evans was involved in a class struggle as much as anything else. An anti-royalist supporter of the French and American revolutions, he came from a background of poverty and was exceedingly unsentimental towards the British crown and his fellow British subjects who manned the Canadian forts during his time with the Mandan tribe on the front line of the Louisiana–Canada border.

It seems strange, therefore, that he took his allegiance to the Spanish king so seriously. My brother, the geographer Dafydd Rhys, takes the view that he fully comprehended the geopolitical implications of his actions on the Canadian border and also realized that by keeping the British crown out of Mandan territory and the future Dakotas he was potentially securing these lands for the revolutionary-minded and expansionist United States of America: 'It is likely enough that Evans served Spain in the conviction that the United States, whose citizens were already pressing westwards towards the Ohio, would inevitably inherit the lands claimed for Spain. Could a Baptist and a radical possibly have thought otherwise? What we do not know is whether John Evans was in touch at any time with the United States authorities. If so, his raising of the Spanish flag in the Mandan villages makes him father of the state of North Dakota rather more by design than accident. Up until then the history of that state has been written from the point of view of those who arrived from the North.'

George Miles of the Beinecke Library also emphasizes the significance that the new Missouri route that Evans traversed brought to the emergent USA: 'If you look at this map, it's striking,' he says. 'It's really not a map of land; it's a map of water. I think of it as being the equivalent of a map of New York City or the London transit system. The reason they're fascinated by all these creeks and all these tributaries is because the way you're going to move goods quickly and efficiently in this time, before the railroad, is by boat. You'll not do it by wagon. So they're fascinated by the water, and the [eventual] ability to get steamboats up the Missouri River means you can get goods there reliably and inexpensively, and that's a big part of how the American hegemony is established in that part of the world, and why the British can't effectively move south from Canada.'

He also sees Evans – Don Juan, that is – in the Hispanic cartographic context of the time. 'I don't know what the perception is in the British Isles about American history, but for most easterners in the United States, for people who grew up east of the Mississippi River, there's always a sense that American history unfolds east to west, and we talk about the Great West, the west frontier, westering movements, but in truth there's also this great movement north. So from New Spain, from Mexico proper, Spanish government and Hispanic-speaking settlers are moving north, so there's this constant kind of expansion or exploration beyond the limits of Spanish settlement that's a northering movement. And I would say from as early as the 1770s until the end of the Mexican Revolution, when Mexico declares independence from Spain, a large part of the Spanish imperial policy is to try to figure out how to protect the northern frontier. You push up the Mississippi and the Missouri because you're worried about the British in Canada, or the French who are left over from New France days, and it's interesting to think of Evans as being connected to that in a way, that his expedition really is a part of that

effort to figure out: what's up there? What do we have on the northern edge of our empire?'

Once he was there, Evans's actions were most dramatic. He forbade
the British Canadians from trading with tribes within the Spanish-
controlled borders and flew a Spanish flag above a formerly British
fort. Many scholars have dwelled on the political implications of this
decisive moment. President Jefferson had a copy of John Evans's map
at the time of the Louisiana Purchase, and as Dafydd Rhys points
out: 'Jefferson decided that the northern boundary of Louisiana and
therefore of the United States must be so drawn as to loop round and
enclose any Missouri drainage which lay north of 49 degrees.' He
continues: 'It would have been difficult for him to argue his case
convincingly without the concrete evidence of John Evans's surveying. Further, had Evans not dislodged the British from amongst the
Mandans in 1796, the British could well have ventured much further
south and the United States–Canada border could have been very
different from what we now know today.'

In his paper 'John Evans and the Geographical Consequences of
Welsh-Speaking Indians', Dafydd Rhys takes this hypothesis to an
extreme by presenting a scenario that outlines the profound destruc-
tive power that myth-making can wield when the benign innocent
tale at its origin morphs out of all recognition and assumes beastly
power:

> How far into history or mythology can we legitimately probe in
> allocating responsibility for the spatial structures of today? Could
> we conceivably blame [the myth of] Madog for the geographical
> consequences of President [George W.] Bush's foreign policy, having
> been elected with a slim, 5 electoral votes majority arguably attribut-
> able to the six electoral votes of Republican-voting North Dakota

and Montana (areas that might now be part of Canada were it not for Evans's actions and contributions)?

From the case of Tony Blair's infamous 'dodgy dossier' on the existence of Iraq's Weapons of Mass Destruction in the build-up to the 2003 war in Iraq, to John Dee's near invention of Madog in the sixteenth century, in the words of Gwyn A. Williams, 'Myth itself can become a historical operative', whether it's true or not. And the consequences of these white lies can often be catastrophic.

Likewise, any canonization of John Evans and his achievements must be measured against the unforeseen consequences of his role as a trader and explorer. Given that he was a Welsh republican revolutionary, looking for an escape route from colonized Wales, there is a great contradiction in his role as a Madog enthusiast, as it validates the idea of colonization as a noble exercise when it is, by its very nature, exploitative. The contradiction is continued when he becomes a representative of the colonial crown of Spain, and in his sympathetic attitude towards the USA and their territorial ambitions over the Native Americans' ancient habitat. His early wish, which he seemingly abandoned, of acting as a Christian missionary amongst the tribes of the Missouri would have violated the cultural autonomy of a people who were already spiritually advanced. Considering that he was deemed to have an honest face, he certainly made a lot of promises to his Mandan hosts that he couldn't ultimately keep, and although this was mostly down to the collapse of the Missouri Company (a circumstance that was out of his hands), he was prone to promise the Earth to people (he never did pay back that twenty-pound loan for his Atlantic passage). It is documented that in September 1804, for example, seven years after Evans's departure from the Mandan nation, Chief Black Cat complained to Lewis and

Clark that Evans had promised to 'return & furnish them with guns & anumition [*sic*] . . .' Of course, it wasn't to be.

His role in the fur trade between the Mandan and Hidatsa tribes and the Canadians, although conducted innocently at a time when there seemed to be an abundance of wildlife on the grasslands of the Great Plains, played a very small part, but a part nevertheless, in the process of industrialization that saw the sustainable nature of the Native American fur trade become the major industry of the booming new city of St Louis, and from the perspective of a wild animal a most exploitative one at that. And his flirtation with freemasonry does not resonate well with the ideals of modern democracy, especially given his revolutionary outlook.

For the most part, however, time and time again we see him as a diligent young pragmatist, experimenting, compromising, bluffing and scheming his way around the emergent West as he desperately, and for the most part heroically, tried to locate the unlikely tribe of the Madogwys against all possible odds.

IEUAN AB IFAN, WELSH REVOLUTIONARY AND ROMANTIC EXPLORER

This is possibly Evans's greatest legacy: his almost transgressive power to defy the logic of what is considered possible in one's lifetime, to complete an impossible journey, to defy what the strict and oppressive class structures of the day could have expected from an orphaned farm labourer. He disregarded the strict parameters of nationality, society and identity, to the point that he fell through the seismic cracks of history as the great colonial powers jostled for supremacy in a continent that's still reeling from the most spectacular pace of change ever witnessed on Earth. In many ways his is a quintessentially American story, that of the heroic individual. He almost fits the rock 'n' roll paradigm 'live fast, die young'.

I ponder: what is that vain lunacy that drives men and women to lose their grip on logical thought and to fantasize of glorious ends? As a relative, it saddens me that the misguided belief in the lost tribe of Madog diverted all the incredible energy and unwavering faith of this remarkably brave young man, and that his life was cut so short by the promise of Empire and mythology. Meditating on this, I contemplate whether this is the central lesson of his life: who needs empires when there's so much to get on with at home? But on the other hand, in following his own nose for adventure, he certainly gave it his all, and now that I have surveyed his journey by mode of investigative concert tour from Wales to the Missouri, and from the 49th parallel to New Orleans, I believe that, ultimately, he is a beautiful example of a historical anomaly, one who defied convention, class structures and even classification itself . . .

EPILOGUE

Voodoo ritual on a Welsh mountain

On a summer's day in Waunfawr we return to the common land on the mountain above John Evans's old cottage at Hafod Olau to deliver his voodoo doll home and to bring to a close my experiment with forces I don't fully comprehend.

Looking out west over the Irish Sea, a strong breeze sweeps through our hair like a pair of busy hands and makes us feel a sense of the immense speed at which the Earth is spinning on its invisible axle. The local community has gathered in front of a shrine, created to the specifications of Kelley, the daughter of the voodoo priestess, and all turn now to watch as my friends Pete and Nigel emerge over the brow of the ridge and pace across the windy grassland, with John on a palanquin, towards the dancers, children, historians, care workers, musicians and employees of Antur Waunfawr who have all gathered in his memory.

The distant waves wink at us as a magical, ad hoc, besuited brass band dance their instruments like drunken partners to a tune that we plucked from the New Orleans gas-light sky on the last night of the tour. It's an ode to the dangers of sailing the treacherous seas of mythology on the *Gwenan Gorn*: the supposed ship that took the mythical Madog and his disciples to a distant land, long ago. Of course, Madog is nothing but a good story that served a political end many moons ago. John Evans, on the other hand, the man who left this simple stone house on a barren hillside and broke through the dreams of romantic Wales into cartographic modernity and the stark, snowy white-out of the upper Badlands, and who died a lonely death far, far away on the swampy banks of the Mississippi, was very, very real.

> Ar y
> Gwenan
> Gorn awn
> rownd yr horn,
> Ar y Gwenan
> Gorn awn rownd yr
> horn,
> Ar y Gwenan
> Gorn.

> Mae tairarddeg llong ac ugain
> bad, Yn cludo'r Cymry i
> brudd ryddhad.

APPENDICES

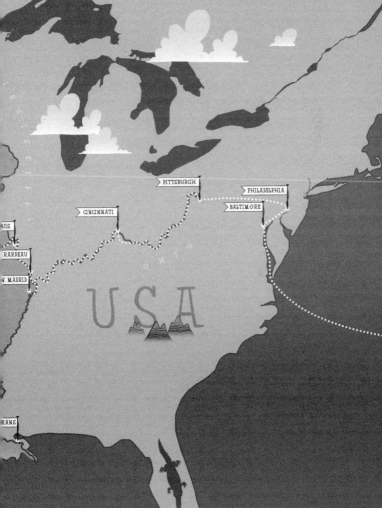

LETTER FROM JOHN EVANS
TO SAMUEL JONES

St Louis July 15th 1797

D.r Sir

Its such a long time since I have departed from
your part of the world that I am ready to suppose every
body of my friends in that Part of the world has given
me up for dead. However after innumerable escapes from
red & white people & undergone and gone Some of the
severest hardships I suppose was ever experienced — I am
by kind providence preserved to have the pleasure of
informing you as well as my other Friends, of some particulars
of Travelies after I left your home I proceded to Fort Pitt
where I was kindly treated by a certain gentleman of the
name of Dr C Wheler for a month to wait for the
high waters from thence we were transported in a few days
to limestone in Kentucky — from there I travelled by land
to bourbon — & from there through the wilderness to
Cincinnata — here I was kindly received by Genl Wilkinson
stayd here a few days — then departed for Louisville
& from thence for New Madrid in Louisiana here
I was kindly received by Mr & Mrs Rus my Country
people — But was obliged to take the oath of allegi
before I could be permitted to debarke — now begins
my life of misery & hardships — in 10 days after my
arrival was taken by a Violent Intermitting fever ——
suceeded by a delirium —— Thank god for friends
for I was paid the greatest attention to
in my Sickness by my kind land lady & all the
great people of the place otherwise I should have
died in the greatest Poverty — Having undertaken the
the voyage of discovery up the Missouri upon the strength
of my own Pockitt which consisted of a dollar & the
Quarter when I left your home — in 2 months my
fever abated a little. my resolution & acuity for proceeding
on my voyage being heightend to such a pitch that I
was determined to risk my life feeble as I was & start
for the Illinois in Company with one man only — neith
of us knew the road — if it could be calld a road for it
was so overgrown with grass that in several places
not the least trace was left — however such as it was
we had the bad fortune to loose it altogether in
the evening of the first day — Now lost in the
infinite wilderness of america — Oh unsufferable think
here is an amusement in Comparison to this —
The parent sun who is so much courted by the northern
nations has in this Distressing moment turnd my Enemy
& threatens to break my brain — like a cake & with dews
from me

the colonial powers liked to carve up the carcass of the Americas arbitrarily, the reality on the ground was that the indigenous tribes were still in charge of large areas of this rapidly changing wilderness, and indeed individual tribes enforced effective trade blockades on rivers such as the Missouri. By and large, the colonial and US governments accepted this fact, and on paper at least the tribes were designated control of vast areas of their ancient homelands where they could continue to hunt and live freely (that these treaties were broken by aggressive expansion is testament to the outlaw reality of the West).

In this era, therefore, when the colonists talked of borders it was in the main of borders concerning trading rights rather than those of sovereign, European-style states. Initially Spain had a blasé attitude to the buffer state of Louisiana; indeed, it had no concrete idea of its size even. But when the British Canadians established trading forts up north at the Mandan villages and along strategic areas of the Missouri River, well within the trading border of Spanish Louisiana in the 1790s, this sent alarm bells ringing all the way to New Orleans, as it could lead not only to an eventual British threat to Mexican lands in the south but also to an end to Spanish dominance of the Missouri fur trade, not to mention shutting off the long-promised north-west passage to the Pacific and trade dominance of the entire continent.

This is why the Mackay–Evans expedition was of such significance to the Spanish government in New Orleans, and why it initially sponsored this otherwise privately funded Missouri Company trading venture. Trade, often based on existing Native American trading routes, was synonymous with power. John Evans's pioneering cartography of the Missouri basin and his capture of the British Canadian fort at the Mandan villages was hugely important to the balance of trading and political power in the region. Within seven years, Spain, sick of the expense of trying to tame the Giant Louisiana Beast, swapped it with France for lands in Europe. New Spain was dead at forty years old. Louisiana was handed back to the French, who sold it immediately to the US for fifteen million dollars, still considered to be one of the best land deals in history. Spain was happy as long as there was a continuing buffer zone between the British in the north and Mexico in the south; it was all the better if they didn't have to maintain it themselves.

In 1804, when the US government's Lewis and Clark expedition followed Evans's 1795–6 Missouri journey, its remit was trade expansion as much as it was discovery. Evans seemingly knew full well the future political significance of repelling British trading interest in the major waterways of the Missouri and Mississippi basin, as it would more than likely facilitate the momentum of US expansion, and with it, or so Evans no doubt hoped, the libertarian values of the American Revolution. Given its prominence in its formative years, it's hardly a surprise that trade became the dominant aspect of American life, on occasion at the expense of liberty itself.

MACKAY'S INSTRUCTIONS TO JOHN EVANS

JAMES MACKAY TO JOHN EVANS, FORT CHARLES (CARLOS), 28 JANUARY 1796

Instructions, given to Jean Evans for crossing the continent in order to discover a passage from the sources of the Missouri to the Pacific Ocean, following the orders of the Director of the company, Don St Yago Clamorgan under the protection of his Excellency Mgr de Baron de Carondelet, Governor-General of the Province of Louisiana, and Mr Zenon Trudeau, Lieutenant-Governor of the Province of Illinois.

During the time of your absence from this place and during your journey to reach the Pacific or any other place, you will observe the following instructions:

Art. 1

From the time of your departure from this fort until your return to the place where I will be living on the Missouri, you will keep a journal of each day and month of the year to avoid any error in the observations of the important journey which you are undertaking. In your journal you will place all that will be remarkable in the country that you will traverse; likewise the route, distance, latitude and longitude, when you observe it, also the winds and weather. You will also keep another journal in which you will make note of all the minerals; vegetables; timber; rocks; flint-stone; territory; production; animals; game; reptiles; lakes; rivers; mountains; portages, with their extent and location; and the different fish and shellfish which the waters may contain. You will insert in the same journal all that may be remarkable and interesting, particularly the different nations; their numbers, manners, customs, government, sentiments, language, religion and all other circumstances relative to their manner of living.

Art. 2

You will take care to mark down your route and distance each day, whether by land or water; in case you will be short of ink, use the powder, and for want of powder, in the summer you will surely find some fruit whose juice can replace both.

Art. 3

In your route from here to the home of the Ponca, trace out as exactly as possible a general route and distance from the Missouri as well as the rivers which fall into it; and although you cannot take the direction of each turn and current of the Missouri, since you go by land, you can mark the general course of the mountains which will be parallel to each bank. You will observe the same thing for every other river [landmark] which you may see during your journey, whether river, lake, ocean or chain of mountains which may effect your observations.

Art. 4

Be very accurate in your observations concerning the nations, their size, their dwellings, their land and their production.

Art. 5

Mr Truteau, our private agent, whom you will find among the Ricara or Mandanes, will give you what you are bound to need. You will consult with him on the most practical route and he will give you guides that he will obtain from the nations where he will be.

Art. 6

You will take for provisions on your route some well-skinned dried meat, which is very nourishing and a very little quantity of which satisfies your appetite as well as your fancy. Always lay up some provisions and keep them for a last resource.

Art. 7

You will take heed not to fall in with some parties of savages, where there are neither women nor children, as they are almost always on the warpath. It would not be prudent to appear at any nation if you can avoid it, unless it be in their villages; and in spite of this be well on your guard. You will never fire any guns except in case of necessity; you will never cut wood except with a knife unless it should be strictly necessary; you will never build a fire without a true need, and you will avoid having the smoke seen from afar, camping if it is possible in the valleys. You will not camp too early and will always leave before daybreak; you will always be on guard against ambushes and will always have your arms in good condition, changing the tinder evening and morning, and you will never separate them from you or place them in the hands of the savages. When you will see some nations, raise your flag a long way off as a sign of peace, and never approach without speaking to them from a distance. When you will enter a village, stop and ground arms at a small distance until they come to receive and conduct you. Appear always on guard and never be fearful or timid, for the savages are not generally bold, but will act in a manner to make you afraid of them. If, however, they see that you are courageous and venturesome they will soon yield to your wishes. You will recollect that the pipe is the symbol of peace and that when they have smoked with you there is no longer any danger; nevertheless you must beware of treason.

On all occasions be reserved with your detachment as well as with the savages; always give to your conduct the air of importance and show good will towards everyone, white or red.

You will carry with you some merchandise, consisting of various small articles suitable for new nations, in order to make presents to the savages which you will discover; but you must be careful of your generosity in this even as in all other things which you carry and bring with you, seeing that the time of your return is uncertain.

Say to the savages whom you will meet on your route that the white people, who come to meet them, speaking of our Company, still have many other kinds of merchandise for them. If they wish to trap some beaver and otter in order to give the skins in exchange for whatever they need, then it is necessary to show them the process of stretching and cleaning them in the same way as all other kinds of peltry are treated.

If you discover some animals which are unknown to us, you will see that you procure some of this kind, alive if possible. There is, they say, on the long chain of the Rockies which you will cross to go to the Pacific Ocean, an animal which has only one horn on its forehead. Be very particular in the description which you will make of it if you will be unable to procure one of this kind.

When you will have crossed the sources of the Missouri and will have gone beyond the Rockies, you will keep as far as possible within the bounds of the 40th degree of north latitude until you will find yourself nearly within the 111th to 112th degree of longitude west meridian of London. Then you will take a northerly direction to the 42nd degree of latitude, always keeping the same longitude in order to avoid the waters, which probably are destined to fall in California. This might induce you to take a route away from the Pacific Ocean. After all, you cannot travel over so great an expanse of land without finding some nations which can inform you about rivers which go towards the setting sun. Then you will build some canoes to descend these rivers, and will watch carefully since there may be some waterfalls on them which can carry you away, since the distance in longitude from the Rockies to the Pacific Ocean ought not to be above 290 leagues, perhaps less, which condition makes it necessary for the rivers to be very rapid or else to have great falls, in comparison with the distance which exists between the sources of the Missouri, which runs over a space of about 1,000 leagues to come to the sea by entering the Mississippi, whose waters are very violent. This is so if it is true that this chain of mountains serves to divide the waters of the west from those of the east.

Mark your route in all places where there will be a portage to pass from one river to another or from one waterfall to another by cutting or notching some trees or by some piles of stones engraved and cut; and take care to place in large letters Charles IV King of Spain and below [that] Company of the Missouri, the day, the month and the year when you do this in order to serve as unquestionable proof of the journey that you are going to make.

There is on the coast of the Pacific Ocean a Russian Settlement that they say is to the north of California, but there is reason to believe that it is not the only one and that the nations of the interior of the continent ought to have knowledge of it. Then, when you will have discovered the places that they inhabit, you will cease to make any sign of taking possession, for fear of having spring up with these foreigners any jealousy which would be prejudicial to the success of your journey. You will not neglect any interesting observation on the seashore and, although there may be some things which do not appear to merit the least attention, nevertheless, in a journey of this nature, everything is sometimes of great importance. Do not fail to measure the risk of the sea in its ebb and flow.

As soon as you will have visited the seashore sufficiently, you will return from it immediately, with as much vigilance as you can, to the place or to the spot where I may be at the time, either among the Mandanes or elsewhere. You will take steps to return by a different route from that which you have taken on your way out if you believe it practical; but mind that if you find the route by which you will have passed rather straight and easy for travelling by water in a canoe or other craft, it will be wiser to return by the same route, and, in case there are portages to make from one river to another or from one rapids to another, see whether the place permits the forming of a settlement.

If, however, you are obliged to search for a new passage to return here from the seashore, you will return from any latitude where you may be when you will take your point of departure to forty-five degrees north latitude; and on your entire route you will examine the most penetrable and practicable places for foreigners to the north country in order to give an account of the means of forming a settlement and fort there to prevent their communication [coming into this territory].

On your journey you will not forget to tell every nation that you discover that their great father, Spain, who is protector of all the white and red men, has sent you to tell them that he has heard of them and their needs and that, desiring to make them happy, he wishes to open a communication to them in order to secure [provide] for them their necessities; that for this purpose it is necessary that all the redskins be peaceful in order that the whites can come to see them; and that, instead of making war, it is better that they should slaughter game with which to feed their women and children.

In your orders be strict with your detachment and take care that no offence is committed against the nations through which you pass, especially by the connection that they may seek to have with the women, a thing which is ordinarily the origin of dissatisfaction and discord with the savages.

Whereas the journey is of very great importance not only to His Catholic Majesty, his subjects and the Company especially, but even [also] to the universe since it ought to open a communication of intercourse through this continent, it requires the clearest evidence to prove the truth of everything and to leave no doubt about the boldness of this discovery.

Take care, above all, to bring with you a collection of the products of the seashore: animals, vegetables, minerals and other curious things that you can find, especially some skirts of sea otters and other sea animals and shellfish which cannot be found in any fresh water. A portion of each will be an unquestionable proof of your journey to the seashore; but, if you can find there any civilized people who wish to give you an affidavit of your journey in whatever language they speak, this will be an additional proof of the validity of your journey.

If on your return, God has disposed of me or I have left the place of my residence on the Missouri, you will not deliver or show to anyone anything relative to your discoveries, but you will go imme-diately to St Louis to deliver all your papers, plans, charts and journals to Monsieur Clamorgan, Director of the Company. In case he is dead or absent, you will deliver them to whoever will represent him at the time, but in the presence of Monsieur Zenon Trudeau, Lieutenant-Governor, or any other who should represent him, keeping in your possession a copy of each thing to be delivered and sent to the said Monsieur Zenon Trudeau by a safe means; this always in case Messieurs Zenon and Clamorgan should be dead or absent.

(Signed) Mackay
Fort Charles, 28 January 1796

NOTES ON TERMINOLOGY
BY AN IGNORANT
EUROPEAN TRAVELLER

Taking a cue from Neil Philip's book *The Great Circle: A History of the First Nations* (2006), in which he states, 'Anyone writing on Native American topics enters a minefield of conflicting names and terms', I would like to offer up my own wish not to offend anyone and also some of the things I have learnt on my journey in the footsteps of John Evans. For example, I previously had no idea that 'Sioux' was an offensive term, coined by their rivals, the Ojibwe tribe, until Edwin Benson corrected me at the Fort Berthold Reservation. He prefers to use the term 'Lakota' (which I've used as a general term on occasion for the multitude of Souian nations – guided again by Neil Philip). Likewise, just as most contemporary tribal names were bastardizations coined by colonial powers, the Mandan nation would sooner be called the 'N'ueta', and the Arikara will soon officially change their name to 'Sahnish'.

For the purpose of clarity, I've made use of these widely known colonial names but have also included revised terminology when I can. This also goes for the name of the 'Welsh', which has been proudly adopted by the majority of its host nation, removing any controversy or stigma from its usage, but which was originally a Germanic word for 'foreigner', coined by the Saxon lowlanders when referring to the Cymry, as we speakers of Welsh, or Cymraeg, instinctively call ourselves.

Whilst Canadians use the term 'First Nations', as I've come to find out, catch-all terms such as 'Native Americans', and 'Indians' (which I was surprised was still so widely used in America), are as bad as each other and highly offensive to many people, so if I have overstepped the mark at any point, please accept my sincerest apologies, in the knowledge that it comes from the ignorance and genuine curiosity of the European tourist rather than from any wish to offend. For the record, I'd be proud to come from anywhere on Earth (or beyond), and my hope in this book has been to celebrate our glorious diversity, continued encounters and cultural exchanges as dwellers of the said planet.

ACKNOWLEDGEMENTS

The emergence of this book has been dependent on an army of friends and family.

Empowered by the enthusiasm and advice of Nemonie Craven Roderick, a literary agent at Jonathan Clowes who bravely thought the proposed book was a rational idea, I set about arranging an investigative concert tour of North America with the aid of Eric Dimenstein in New York City's DUMBO district under the Manhattan Bridge. Never did he flinch at its possibly whimsical nature. Thanks also to Nicole Roeder and all the staff at Ground Control Touring. On that tour and film adventure, many of the interviews that were transcribed into this book were arranged by Catryn Ramasut and Kelly Pickard, both of whom were instrumental in the logistics, as was the legend of the frontier Joe Puleo, who had the greatest number of sleepless nights and the hardest trucking routes. I'm forever indebted to him for my appreciation of the joys of American coffee and frozen custard (consumed separately). Dylan Goch, who directed the film of this book, came to the rescue of many slow (speaking for myself) interviews by placing considered questions to the interviewee that often led to more revealing answers than I could ever fish out and which provided a great resource for this book.

Haydn Jones and Menna Jones at Antur Waunfawr gave me great

assistance in providing copies of documents relating to John Evans when they had much more important things to be doing.

This is also true of my family: my brother Dafydd turned me on in particular to the work of W. Raymond Wood, and his own essay on John Evans, 'The Geographical Consequences of Welsh Indians', contains some of the profoundest insights into Evans's legacy that have been written. His guidance was crucial, as was the generosity of my sister, Non, and mother, Margaret, in sharing details and documents of our familial link with Evans. As to all the other living relatives of John Evans, I hope this book brings neither heavy burden nor distress, and my sincerest apologies if I seem to have misrepresented any aspect of his memory in any way.

My huge thanks to Simon Prosser at Hamish Hamilton for his enthusiasm in sharing this story and for guiding me through the mysterious process of producing a book, and also to the expertise and rigour of the copy-editor, Caroline Pretty, Janette Revill's text design, Rachael Tremlett's shaped poems, Paul Nicholas's map of John Evans's journey to the American Interior, and the excitement and support of Anna Kelly, Ellie Smith, Nathan Hull and Matt Clacher.

One of my biggest thank-yous is to all the interviewees, most of whom have left a lasting impression on me. I hope my depictions of you are not too painful. This book would be half its size without you. A great big thanks to Edwin Benson, Marilin Hudson, Calvin Grinell and Keith Bear, too, for opening doors at the Fort Berthold Reservation, and to the great generosity of Cory Spotted Bear at Twin Buttes, whose blankets and coats keep us warm here in Wales. Likewise to Dennis Hastings, Margery Coffee and Richard for their warm welcome in the Omaha Reservation. An extra thank-you to the mayor of Rio Grande, for his incredible hospitality and the mobilization of the police force!

Acknowledgements

The historical aspects of this book are largely dependent on the previous scholarly acrobatics of the Welsh historian David Williams, his American counterpart A. P. Nasatir, and their academic heirs on both sides of the Atlantic: Gwyn A. Williams and W. Raymond Wood. Beyond my insights as a relative, and an advantage in reading Welsh-language papers and some minor discoveries in the Archivo de Indias in Seville, I have unearthed very little new academic material on John Evans, as the documents concerning his story have already been pored over and analysed thoroughly by the professional historians mentioned. This has, however, been an opportunity for me to compile and update the story so far. And as W. Raymond Wood told me, some things need repetition to survive. I would like to thank him for coming to see the show and for his time in Columbia, and also to acknowledge in lieu of a bibliography that the diplomatic flurry of letters between Evans and the Canadian traders were reproduced from his compilation of documents in his book *Prologue to Lewis and Clark: The Mackay and Evans Expedition* (2003). I also rely on Wood's book, in many cases, for my quotation from journals and letters. Wood cites A. P. Nasatir's *Before Lewis and Clark: Documents Illustrating the History of the Missouri, 1785–1804* (1952) as his own source in many cases, and I too have relied on Nasatir's scholarship. In the case of the documents from the hands of Truteau and Gayoso de Lemos, I cite translations from *Before Lewis and Clark* that were likely made by Annie Heloise Abel and Nasatir himself, respectively. I refer to the journals of Lewis and Clark as edited by Bernard DeVoto (1953). I have occasionally amended sources. Statistics and history relating to the Omaha tribe were collated thanks to The Omaha Tribe Historical Research Project. All documents are printed as originally written.

Acknowledgements

I would also like to thank Alun Llwyd and Kevin Tame from Turnstile Music for coordinating the investigative concert tour, the recording and everything in between.

I would like to thank Huw Evans, Cate Timothy, Alan Lane and Gill Boden for letting me write at their homes, and for babysitting, as did Tamsin, Steve, Noi and Arlene. But mostly I would like to thank and dedicate this book to Catryn, Mali Mai and Mabli.

I would also like to thank the following: Pete Fowler for the beautiful title font of this book and the cover itself; Louise Evans for making the avatar of John Evans from Pete's design; Kliph Scurlock, Doug McKinney and Jessica Wisneski; Ryan Owen Eddleston was very much part of the making of this book, as was Dom Corbisiero, who recorded the interviews; Nate Krenkel, Conor Oberst and Mike Mogis for demystifying Omaha; and thanks to Siôn Glyn for the books. How could I not thank Steve Rajewski and Brett Padget for the fantastic drives on the trail of Evans, and Jon Savage for providing the soundtracks to those drives as well as John Evans's astrological details. Many thanks to all the kind people at the Beinecke library, Yale, for their help with this project and also for the pizza. Thanks also to Dafydd Ieuan, Huw Bunford, Cian Ciaran, Guto Pryce, Rhodri Puw, Dewi Emlyn for previous American adventures, and to the memory of Les Morrison whose enthusiasm formed lasting friendships on that great continent.

AMERICAN-INTERIOR.COM

He just wanted a decent book to read ...

Not too much to ask, is it? It was in 1935 when Allen Lane, Managing Director of Bodley Head Publishers, stood on a platform at Exeter railway station looking for something good to read on his journey back to London. His choice was limited to popular magazines and poor-quality paperbacks – the same choice faced every day by the vast majority of readers, few of whom could afford hardbacks. Lane's disappointment and subsequent anger at the range of books generally available led him to found a company – and change the world.

'We believed in the existence in this country of a vast reading public for intelligent books at a low price, and staked everything on it'
Sir Allen Lane, 1902–1970, founder of Penguin Books

The quality paperback had arrived – and not just in bookshops. Lane was adamant that his Penguins should appear in chain stores and tobacconists, and should cost no more than a packet of cigarettes.

Reading habits (and cigarette prices) have changed since 1935, but Penguin still believes in publishing the best books for everybody to enjoy. We still believe that good design costs no more than bad design, and we still believe that quality books published passionately and responsibly make the world a better place.

So wherever you see the little bird – whether it's on a piece of prize-winning literary fiction or a celebrity autobiography, political tour de force or historical masterpiece, a serial-killer thriller, reference book, world classic or a piece of pure escapism – you can bet that it represents the very best that the genre has to offer.

Whatever you like to read – trust Penguin.

read more
www.penguin.co.uk